Women
Inventors

Other Books in the History Makers Series:

History **MAKERS**

Women Inventors

By Stephen Currie

Lucent Books
P.O. Box 289011, San Diego, CA 92198-9011

Library of Congress Cataloging-in-Publication Data

Currie, Stephen, 1960–
  Women Inventors / by Stephen Currie.
    p. cm. — (History makers)
  Includes bibliographical references and index.
  ISBN 1-56006-865-5
  1. Women inventors—Biography—Juvenile literature. [1. Inventors.
2. Women—Biography.] I. Title. II. Series.
  T39.C87 2001
  609.2'2—dc21

                                              00-12663

Cover Photos: (center) Madam Walker's beauty school, (top) Grace Hopper, (bottom, right) Temple Grandin, (bottom, left) Rose O'Neill

Printed in the U.S.A.

CONTENTS

FOREWORD

The literary form most often referred to as "multiple biography" was perfected in the first century A.D. by Plutarch, a perceptive and talented moralist and historian who hailed from the small town of Chaeronea in central Greece. His most famous work, *Parallel Lives*, consists of a long series of biographies of noteworthy ancient Greek and Roman statesmen and military leaders. Frequently, Plutarch compares a famous Greek to a famous Roman, pointing out similarities in personality and achievements. These expertly constructed and very readable tracts provided later historians and others, including playwrights like Shakespeare, with priceless information about prominent ancient personages and also inspired new generations of writers to tackle the multiple biography genre.

The Lucent History Makers series proudly carries on the venerable tradition handed down from Plutarch. Each volume in the series consists of a set of five to eight biographies of important and influential historical figures who were linked together by a common factor. In *Rulers of Ancient Rome*, for example, all the figures were generals, consuls, or emperors of either the Roman Republic or Empire; while the subjects of *Fighters Against American Slavery*, though they lived in different places and times, all shared the same goal, namely the eradication of human servitude. Mindful that politicians and military leaders are not (and never have been) the only people who shape the course of history, the editors of the series have also included representatives from a wide range of endeavors, including scientists, artists, writers, philosophers, religious leaders, and sports figures.

Each book is intended to give a range of figures—some well known, others less known; some who made a great impact on history, others who made only a small impact. For instance, by making Columbus's initial voyage possible, Spain's Queen Isabella I, featured in *Women Leaders of Nations*, helped to open up the New World to exploration and exploitation by the European powers. Unarguably, therefore, she made a major contribution to a series of events that had momentous consequences for the entire world. By contrast, Catherine II, the eighteenth-century Russian queen, and Golda Meir, the modern Israeli prime minister, did not play roles of global impact; however, their policies and actions significantly influenced the historical development of both their own countries and their regional neighbors. Regardless of their relative importance in the greater historical scheme, all of the figures chronicled in the History Makers series made contributions to posterity; and their public achievements, as well as what is known about their private lives, are presented and evaluated in light of the most recent scholarship.

In addition, each volume in the series is documented and substantiated by a wide array of primary and secondary source quotations. The primary source quotes enliven the text by presenting eyewitness views of the times and culture in which each history maker lived; while the secondary source quotes, taken from the works of respected modern scholars, offer expert elaboration and/ or critical commentary. Each quote is footnoted, demonstrating to the reader exactly where biographers find their information. The footnotes also provide the reader with the means of conducting additional research. Finally, to further guide and illuminate readers, each volume in the series features photographs, two bibliographies, and a comprehensive index.

The History Makers series provides both students engaged in research and more casual readers with informative, enlightening, and entertaining overviews of individuals from a variety of circumstances, professions, and backgrounds. No doubt all of them, whether loved or hated, benevolent or cruel, constructive or destructive, will remain endlessly fascinating to each new generation seeking to identify the forces that shaped their world.

Women Who Invent

There is much debate over the identity of America's first woman inventor. Some say it was a Connecticut native named Mary Kies, who, in 1809, patented a method of weaving straw. Others contend that it was Sybilla Masters of Philadelphia. In 1715 Masters's husband received an English patent for a machine that cleaned and cured Indian corn; the patent, however, referred to the "new Invencon [invention] found out by Sybilla, his wife."[1] Perhaps the first American woman inventor was Mrs. Samuel Slater, first name unknown, who developed a type of sewing thread in 1793. Or, conceivably, Betsy Metcalf of Rhode Island, who found a way of braiding straw five years later but never applied for a patent on her idea.

Or, perhaps, the first woman inventor was none of these people. In some ways, it is impossible to tell who was the first woman inventor in America. The confusion stems partly from sketchy records and the many years that have passed since these women lived. It also stems from questions about the precise definition of *inventor*. To some observers, an inventor is someone who holds a patent—essentially a copyright that gives the inventor the exclusive right to develop and market the invention commercially. In this view, Slater and Kies have priority over Masters and Metcalf.

Others agree with the basic definition but add a twist: Masters, they argue, was a victim of living in a time during which no woman was thought capable of inventing. The mere fact that her name was not formally listed on the patent should not eliminate her from being called America's first woman to hold a patent. However, this definition, although perhaps fairer than the first, has problems of its own. Sybilla Masters may not have been the first wife to see her husband get credit for an invention she developed. It is entirely possible that several woman inventors have disappeared completely from history in just this way.

A third definition does not look at patents at all but simply asks who first developed a new and useful device. That brings Metcalf back into the running. Unfortunately, this definition also adds another layer of confusion. Although the U.S. government has information relating to the millions of American inventions that have been patented, there is no central location for inventions that have not. Thus, it is entirely possible that some clever inventor preceded any of the four listed above.

Little Known as Inventors

The question of who was the first American woman to invent points out some of the issues regarding women and inventions in general. American women have, in fact, been creative and persistent inventors over the years. Women have patented knitting machines, flares, even an automatic pistol. Although many of these devices and methods have long since been forgotten or have been replaced by better and cheaper alternatives, some have had an enormous impact on society.

Most Americans, however, are unaware of the depth and breadth of women's inventiveness. The reasons for this are many. On occasion—as was true with Sybilla Masters—men have taken the credit for inventions actually devised by women. In 1935, for example, Max Landsman patented an umbrella with a window through which a pedestrian could look out into traffic while still staying dry. The idea, however, actually came from his wife, Eva, who had been hit by a car during a rainstorm. Max did indeed turn Eva's idea into something patentable, but her role in the process appears nowhere on the patent. In a similar vein, some argue that Eli Whitney's invention of the cotton gin was actually the work of his boss, plantation owner Katherine Greene, though evidence to support the contention is sketchy.

Other women were leery of patenting their inventions under their own names. They deliberately asked a man to stand in as the official patentee, or they hid their gender by using only initials in place of first names. One nineteenth-century patent commissioner suggested that women should do exactly that. "If [a certain invention] had been known [as] the invention of a woman," he argued, "it would have been regarded as a failure."[2] Prejudice against women was rampant throughout the nineteenth century and well into the twentieth. To put a woman's name on an invention—especially one not specifically intended for women's spheres of family and home— was seen by many as a commercial kiss of death, and many women preferred money to credit.

Finally, prejudice over the years has steered women away from the process of inventing. Although not all inventors have scientific backgrounds, many do—and until quite recently only a relative handful of women entered the technical fields of engineering, chemistry, and physics, in which the largest share of inventions were produced. To some extent, avoidance of these fields was by choice. In many cases, however, even those women who were interested were barred from attending school, taking lessons, or working in areas that fit their passions. The result, over the years, has been a scarcity of women trying to invent. One recent writer on women inventors, for instance, speaks of a patent attorney who says that, in forty years of practice, he has never represented a woman.

Yet it is clear that women have been able inventors when given the time, inclination, and opportunity. And in light of how little known many of the inventors are, a surprising number of these in-

Captain Grace M. Hopper (standing) discusses an aspect of computing with a staff member. Hopper is credited with inventing the compiler, used in computer programming.

ventions have proved tremendously useful in today's world. Some have made a major difference in the lives of many people while others have made daily life that much easier. Correction fluid, for example, was the invention of a woman, Bette Nesmith Graham. So was Kevlar, used in manufacturing bulletproof vests; it was the creation of a chemist named Stephanie Kwolek. Nobel Prize–winner Gertrude Elion is one of many women to earn patents on new and valuable medications; Harriet Strong created technology to make dams stronger; Amanda Theodosia Jones improved canning techniques, thereby keeping food fresher for longer. The women whose lives are detailed in the following chapters are five among many American women who have created something useful and new.

CHAPTER 1

Temple Grandin

Many scientists and inventors have overcome remarkably long odds to create the theories and inventions that made them famous. Thomas Edison, for example, began to lose his hearing by the age of seven. Labeled unteachable and possibly mentally retarded, he was expelled from school. Albert Einstein, similarly, was slow to speak as a child and had to support himself as a clerk for several years before his scientific ability became widely recognized.

But the story of Temple Grandin is perhaps even more impressive. Although suffering from autism, a disorder that makes normal life virtually impossible for most of its victims, Grandin not only managed to make her way in the world but also succeeded brilliantly in her chosen career. A professor, business owner, and consultant, Grandin is best known for a number of inventions that changed the cattle industry. And in some ways she succeeded in creating these inventions not despite her disabilities but because of them.

Early Problems

From the time she was six months old, it was clear that something was the matter with Grandin. Born in Boston on August 29, 1947, Grandin seemed perfectly normal at first. Indeed, over the first few weeks of her life she progressed more or less normally. Before long, however, Grandin's response to typical infant stimulation had begun to change noticeably. Whereas most young babies enjoy being held and learn to cuddle and hug, Grandin resisted whenever adults tried to hold her. At the age of only a few months, she tensed her muscles when she was picked up, making her body stiff and rigid. Soon she began lashing out at adults who touched her, turning on them violently as if they were enemies. "I was like a little wild animal,"[3] she remembers, looking back on her early childhood.

As Grandin got older, the problems grew worse. She was an extremely difficult toddler. Tantrums were common; so were destructive behaviors. "I chewed up puzzles and spit the cardboard mush out on the floor," she said years later. "I had a violent temper, and when thwarted, I'd throw anything handy."[4] Language was another issue. At the age of two, Grandin had essentially no language skills. She spoke no words—indeed, she made few noises other than screams—and showed no understanding of what anyone said to her. Her parents feared that she might be deaf, but the results of a hearing test indicated that deafness was not the problem.

As it turned out, Grandin suffered from autism, a brain disorder that impairs a person's ability to connect with others. How autism reveals itself varies widely according to the person and the severity of the disorder. Some autistic people are mentally retarded; others are of normal or even superior intelligence. Some are subject to seizures, but others are not. Some people with autism have obvious neurological problems, such as repeating the same physical gesture again and again; meanwhile others appear completely normal at first glance.

Temple Grandin lectures to an audience on the subject of autism, a brain disorder that impairs a person's ability to connect with others.

Autism

Several features, however, are common to all cases of autism. Most notable among these is a sense of aloneness. It is hard for autistic people to empathize with others or even at times to recognize or acknowledge others' existence. People with autism "do not make eye contact," noted Austrian scientist Hans Asperger, one of the first doctors to describe autism in children. Asperger had also identified several other related hallmarks of autism: abnormal or nonexistent language skills, a lack of impulse control, and the absence of any true emotion. "There is a poverty of facial expressions and gestures,"[5] Asperger wrote. Indeed, autism is diagnosed by careful observation rather than through blood tests, brain scans, or DNA samples. Most often, a neurologist or other doctor observes the child carefully, takes a medical history, and diagnoses based on that information.

Today a large number of autistic children are kept at home with their families. Many attend schools in their own districts, and some are even mainstreamed into "regular" classrooms. Given intensive academic and social support, a few succeed well beyond expectations. During Grandin's childhood, however, most children diagnosed as autistic ended up in an institution. The disorder was considered not only incurable but also unmanageable; the few parents who attempted to raise their autistic children themselves were counseled to do otherwise.

Grandin's mother, though, strongly disagreed with those who tried to have her child institutionalized. She insisted on keeping Grandin at home, and she did her best to provide a rich learning environment for her daughter. She also surrounded Grandin with professionals who could help her move beyond the limitations her autism imposed. "Mother had a knack for recognizing which people could help me and which ones could not,"[6] Grandin says today. Instead of relegating her daughter to an institution, Grandin's mother found patient teachers, knowledgeable doctors, and determined speech therapists who would do their best to ensure that Grandin continued to make progress.

Despite the help from these and other concerned adults, Grandin found life as an autistic child and teenager far from easy. She did eventually learn to speak, read, and write, and she did quite well in some academic subjects, notably science. Nevertheless, like many people with neurological problems, Grandin found certain cognitive tasks extremely difficult. Math, she remembers, was almost impossible. French, if anything, was worse. Even in English, pronouns and prepositions made little sense to her, so she regularly left them out while reading—sometimes missing the point of the text as she did.

Abstract nouns were hard for her to understand, as were verbs that did not lend themselves easily to a concrete picture. "To this day certain verb conjugations, such as 'to be,' are absolutely meaningless to me,"[7] Grandin says.

Social Differences

Grandin's academic difficulties, though, were not as severe as the social difficulties she faced. Through much of elementary and high school she was the butt of constant teasing, in part the result of her odd behavior. Nicknamed "Tape Recorder" because of her tendency—fairly common among autistic children—to repeat the same sentences again and again, Grandin withdrew into her own private world. "I knew I did not fit in with my high school peers," she says, "and I was unable to figure out what I was doing wrong. No matter how hard I tried, they made fun of me."[8]

It was not until many years later that Grandin began to understand how her autism had set her apart from other people. Perhaps the most important reason was that her autism limited the depths of her emotion. "I get great satisfaction out of doing clever things with my mind," she once wrote, "but I don't know what it is like to feel rapturous joy."[9] The same was true with sadness, anger, or excitement. Grandin had great difficulty empathizing with others, even fictional characters in books, and she could not understand some of the more subtle feelings that motivate most people. To survive in a socially complex world, of course, she had to learn some of the language that accompanies these emotions. Doing so, however, was far from easy. "Much of the time I feel like an anthropologist on Mars,"[10] she said, likening the task to a normal person trying to make sense of the behavior of extraterrestrials.

Other Factors

Almost as important as Grandin's emotional difficulties were the complicated workings of her senses. Many people may find the noise of a vacuum cleaner annoying or the touch of sandpaper irritating. A person with autism, however, may be completely unable to shut out these sensations and may, indeed, find them literally painful. As a result, people with autism can be in an almost constant state of distress. At the very least, they find themselves easily distracted.

Although Grandin was less impaired in this regard than many other autistic people, she always found some sounds and sensations extremely annoying—and impossible to ignore. "When I was in college," she writes, "my roommate's hair dryer sounded like a jet plane taking off."[11] Likewise, Grandin found new clothes agonizingly scratchy against her skin, and she could barely stand the sensation of shampooing her hair.

The third factor that pushed Grandin apart from her peers involved her thought processes. Whereas most people think in words or in a combination of words and pictures, Grandin thought exclusively in visual images. In part, this reliance on visual pictures was what made short, nonspecific words like *of* and *is* so difficult for her to understand; finding a concrete picture to represent them was next to impossible. Indeed, Grandin says, "Words are like a second language to me. I translate both spoken and written words into full-color movies, complete with sound, which run like a VCR tape in my head. When someone speaks to me, his words are instantly translated into pictures."[12] Grandin's difficulty with others partly stemmed from the fact that most people were primarily language-based thinkers and she was not. What seemed logical and reasonable to them did not necessarily make sense to her.

A Positive Force

A lack of emotion, a tendency to think in pictures, an unusual sensitivity to stimulation—all of these characteristics made Grandin's life much more difficult than it might have been had she not been born autistic. At the same time, however, Grandin did not see her autism as a completely negative force. In her view, autism may actually create interesting and original thinkers. As she wrote in 1990, "If the genes that caused these conditions were eliminated there might be a terrible price to pay. It is possible that persons with bits of these traits are more creative, or possibly even geniuses. . . . If science eliminated these genes, maybe the whole world would be taken over by accountants."[13]

Regardless of whether Grandin's overall quality of life would have been improved by removing her autism, there is no doubt that her disorder helped her create the inventions for which she is best known—a series of designs for cattle ramps, feed lots, slaughterhouses, and other aspects of farm animal management. The link between her autism and this work is both clear and surprisingly personal. Grandin's ideas for these designs stemmed directly from her experiences as a child, when hugs, cuddling, and other touches represented an unbearable sensory overload.

However, Grandin made an important distinction between unwanted touches and touches she instigated on her own. Whereas unexpected touches came as a shock to her system, that was far from true when she knew they were coming. Indeed, in some ways

Grandin reaches into a cattle containment area. Personal experience with autism led her to make discoveries that were advantageous in handling cattle.

she craved pressure against her skin, as long as the idea was hers. "When I was six," she remembers, "I would wrap myself up in blankets and get under sofa cushions, because the pressure was relaxing."[14]

The Squeeze Chute

For some years Grandin continued to seek out small, tight places when she was feeling especially anxious. She daydreamed, too, about the possibility of building some kind of pressure machine, one that would supply exactly as much sensation to her body as she wanted, when she wanted it. The machine remained simply a dream, however, until the summer before her senior year of high school, when she visited an aunt who lived on an Arizona ranch. There, Grandin saw a squeeze chute, a device that was used to hold cattle and steady them to receive vaccinations.

The chute worked simply enough. Cattle were driven into the chute one at a time. As they moved forward, the chute narrowed. After the cattle had gone a few yards, side panels pressed up against them, cutting off their ability to maneuver. At the same time, metal bars restrained their heads. The purpose was to keep the animals still, as in a clamp, so the vaccinations could be given quickly and easily. Grandin, however, related the squeeze chute to her own life. She noted that the pressure seemed to calm some of the animals. Nervous when they entered the chute, they appeared much more relaxed when the panels were pressing tightly against their flanks.

Taken with the idea that the chute had a calming effect, Grandin got her aunt's permission to try it out on herself. Although she initially felt fearful as the passage narrowed around her, Grandin soon discovered that the chute worked exactly as she had hoped it would. "For about an hour afterward I felt very calm and serene," she remembered years later. "My constant anxiety had diminished. This was the first time I ever felt really comfortable in my own skin."[15]

Upon returning to her home, Grandin constructed a similar machine. Her visual approach to life served her well; she designed her own squeeze machine based on what she had seen at her aunt's ranch and built it herself out of plywood panels. Her first versions provided lots of pressure—so much pressure, in fact, that the machine caused her pain. Over the years Grandin refined, redesigned, and rebuilt her squeeze machine to reduce the pain and increase the comfort. Although over time she came to need it less and less, she continued to find it useful in times of stress.

Scientific Validation

Designing and building the squeeze machine was quite an accomplishment for a young person, especially one with so many difficulties managing ordinary life. Many adults who knew Grandin, however, focused less on the accomplishment and more on several concerns the machine raised in their minds. Some feared the machine would encourage her to withdraw when the world became difficult. Others wondered if the pressure was really what she needed, and many thought it was just plain strange. Fortunately for Grandin, a few adults in her life saw that it seemed to benefit her.

Most notable among these was William Carlock, one of Grandin's high school science teachers and an important mentor in her life. Carlock not only defended her use of the squeeze machine but also challenged her to learn more about it. If she kept up her studies, he assured her, she could learn enough about science to know why pressure was so relaxing. "Instead of taking my weird device away," she recalls, "he used it to motivate me to study, get good grades, and go to college."[16]

Through a combination of listening to her teacher and a desire to prove the other adults wrong, Grandin threw herself into science at the end of high school and in college as well. As far as she was concerned, the benefits of the squeeze machine were obvious. She kept it in plain sight in her dormitory room throughout her time at college, unwilling to hide its existence or to apologize for using it.

But at the same time, several psychologists and psychiatrists were trying to convince her to eliminate the machine from her life. To

Grandin applied the benefits that she experienced with her squeeze machine (pictured) to the process of herding cattle.

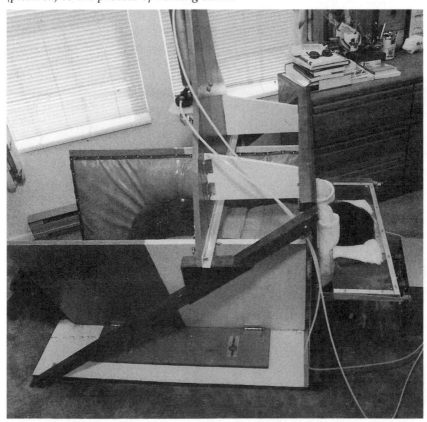

prove them wrong, Grandin read all she could about pressure and autism. In her methodical, concrete way, she sought proof that deep pressure really did calm autistic people. As one interviewer puts it, she was "determined to find a scientific 'validation' of her feelings."[17]

Grandin completed college in 1970, graduating with a bachelor's degree in psychology. Five years later she received a master's degree in animal science; she would eventually earn a doctoral degree as well. As Grandin worked her way through college and graduate school, the question of pressure and its link to autism occupied much of her time. Her research tended to confirm the value of her invention. Much of what she discovered was published in scientific essays and was checked by other scientists.

Today experts increasingly agree that deep pressure, such as that provided by a squeeze machine, does indeed help calm many neurologically impaired people. Some of Grandin's own designs have been produced commercially and are currently used in the treatment of children with autism. Although there is still plenty of debate involving how many children can be helped by machines such as this—and how much those children actually benefit—Grandin cer-

While Grandin pursued her education, she remained focused on the link between pressure and autism.

tainly has gathered enough evidence to prove the squeeze machine's benefit for herself.

Animals

Grandin's research into squeeze machines led her in another direction as well, this time in her capacity as a consultant and a professor. Soon after completing her master's degree, Grandin founded her own consulting firm, Grandin Livestock Handling Systems, and since 1990 she has worked as a professor of animal science at Colorado State University. As a consultant and a professor, Grandin investigated the effect of pressure on animals and came to a surprising conclusion: In their reactions to deep pressure, animals such as cattle and pigs were quite similar to Grandin and other autistic people.

In fact, as Grandin researched the issue, she began to believe that people with autism were like certain farm animals in more ways than just their response to pressure. For example, they seemed especially alike in their general responses to sensory stimulation. "Cattle are disturbed by the same sorts of sounds as autistic people," she notes. "A light touch will make them pull away, a firm touch calms them. The way I would pull away from being touched is the way a wild cow will pull away—getting me used to being touched is very similar to taming a wild cow."[18] Grandin has said that her own sensory life has more in common with those of animals than it does with the experiences of people without neurological problems.

Moreover, Grandin came to believe that the emotional lives of autistic people mirrored those of cattle. Like cows, she realized, people with autism tend to be jumpy and quick to feel that their personal space is being invaded. Again like cows, they have trouble adapting to change. Even sensory overload may have a connection to the animal world. "Could this be an old antipredator instinct that has surfaced?" Grandin wonders. "In the wild, a broken branch on a tree or disturbed earth is a possible sign of predator activity in the vicinity."[19] For a cow, paying attention to everything helps the animal and its species survive. In a nonprey species such as humans, however, such concerns can get in the way of healthy functioning.

Grandin's discovery of the sensory and emotional similarities between autistic people and certain animals was not simply of academic interest. Instead, Grandin realized she could apply her knowledge and research to problems of animal care. People who work with large animals, Grandin knew, often need to keep the animals stationary. Vaccinations are a good example: As Grandin had noticed when she visited her aunt, the cattle were forced into the chute and were held immobile while they were given their shots. Another example is the slaughterhouse, where cattle are herded into a chute similar to a squeeze chute and are kept still while they are killed.

Putting the Pieces Together

However, Grandin was bewildered and sometimes appalled by the way many commercial squeeze chutes and other holding devices controlled the animals. At feed lots, ranches, and slaughterhouses across the United States, Grandin watched workers wielding whips and electric prods herd frightened, panicked cattle into tight and unpleasant places.

There had to be a better way, Grandin reasoned. It seemed to her that it should be possible to keep the cattle still without terrifying them. That was especially true of the animals immobilized for vaccinations or other similar purposes, animals who would live through their experience. There was no point in scaring them needlessly. Rather than traumatizing their cattle, people should instead do their best to keep them calm—thereby improving the quality of their lives.

Finding a different way would also be better for the cattle that were killed, Grandin soon realized. The methods used in the slaughter represented a terrible way for cattle to die. As she later wrote about one Midwestern plant she had visited,

> Employees wearing football helmets attached a nose tong to the nose of a writhing beast suspended by a chain wrapped around one back leg. Each terrified animal was forced with an electric prod to run into a small stall which had a slick floor on a forty-five degree angle. This caused the animal to slip and fall so that workers could attach the chain to its rear leg. As I watched this nightmare, I thought "This should not be happening in a civilized society." I vowed that I would replace [this] plant from hell with a kinder and gentler system.[20]

Deeply concerned about the welfare of the animals, Grandin set out to design a better method of restraint. In planning her designs, Grandin drew partly on common sense. Many systems in existence early in Grandin's career had features that needlessly scared or hurt the animals. Some had loud clanking gates or bars that descended with a screech. Others had conveyor belts that did not adequately support the animal or walls with sharp metal edges that dug into the cattle's sides. Much of Grandin's early work focused on redesigning those parts of the machines.

Cattle move within the curved chute with high solid sides. This design, created by Grandin, helps keep cattle calm in the slaughterhouse.

But Grandin also drew on her own experiences as an autistic person to reform the industry. Her need for a squeeze machine of her own helped her empathize with the cattle and think more carefully about their needs than most other people would have done. Moreover, since Grandin's own sensory system and emotional makeup were so much like those of cows, she reasoned, her reactions to holding systems would probably be similar as well. "Being autistic has helped me understand how they feel,"[21] Grandin later summed up.

As a result, Grandin was able to examine the whole question of animal restraint from a cow's perspective. "I've often seen her where the animals are, trying to envision how the animals might feel and what they might be thinking,"[22] says a veterinarian friend. Grandin spent weeks photographing the entrances to chutes, looking for visual patterns that disturbed her nervous system. That which disturbed her, she reasoned, would probably disturb the animals as well. She also listened at feed lots and slaughterhouses for sounds unnoticed by most workers—but distracting to her and in all likelihood to the cattle, too. "You've got to get down and look right up the chute to see what the animal is seeing,"[23] she explains.

Finally, Grandin used careful observation and carried out studies to determine in what circumstances cattle were most likely to be calm. The standard design for a chute, for example, was long and straight. Grandin changed that, realizing that cows naturally veer to one side as they come together in a herd. Her chute designs curved to take advantage of this instinct. Grandin noticed, too, that many chutes forced cattle down slopes so steep that the animals became anxious; she smoothed the path, reducing their anxiety. Likewise, Grandin realized that cattle are most soothed when they can rest their heads against one another's bodies. Her designs eliminated spacing between the cattle and allowed them to touch one another as they moved through the chute—again with a noticeable calming effect.

Grandin argued that cattle chutes should be narrow enough for the animals to touch one another, thereby reducing their anxiety.

Grandin's methods seemed to be successful for cattle who were going to be slaughtered as well as for those who were simply going for veterinary treatment. "In some plants," she writes,

> the cattle remain absolutely calm and the employees are very conscientious. At one large plant, 240 cattle per hour quietly walked up the ramp and voluntarily entered. . . . It was as if they were going in to get milked. Each fat steer walked into the restrainer entrance and settled down on the conveyor like a little old lady getting on the bus. Most animals entered the restrainer when they were patted on the rear end. Since the cattle move through the system on a continuous line, they are never alone and separated from their buddies.[24]

Reaction

Though Grandin's ideas had both common sense and research behind them, they were not easily accepted within the meat and ranching industries. Her early designs were ignored; her consulting business, in which she advised farmers, meatpackers, and others involved with cattle on effective chute designs, got off to a very slow start.

Part of the problem had to do with Grandin herself. The meat industry was dominated by men, often from a Western ranching background. As a woman originally from the East Coast, Grandin was already viewed with suspicion by conservative ranchers and plant managers. Adding to the problem was Grandin's autism, which many people interpreted as unfriendliness or something close to insanity. Instead of listening with an open mind as she described the problems of the systems they were using, they were likely to resent her interference in their business.

Another issue was that many people in the industry did not see a strong reason for change. They wondered what difference it made whether a steer was calm or panicked when it was killed. Some reasoned that the industry was by its very nature brutal and violent: Regardless of its emotions, the animal would very soon be dead. Why spend money to replace a system that served its purpose? Grandin encountered similar opposition regarding veterinary chutes and other types of inventions that did not end in the animals' deaths. Animals were not humans, some ranchers pointed out; they did not feel pain and emotion the same way that people did, and therefore major changes in chutes and other holding systems were unnecessary.

By pointing out the economic benefits of her restraint designs, Grandin won over even those who were emphatically opposed to changing livestock handling systems.

Grandin, however, continued to plug away. In this, her autism may actually have been helpful; lacking the emotions of embarrassment or self-consciousness, she did not especially care what others thought of her. She worked tirelessly to promote her designs, and bit by bit she began to win over those who opposed her. Often all she needed was a chance to be heard. When meatpackers, veterinarians, and ranchers looked past her gender and autism and saw how much she actually knew about cattle, they began to treat her with more respect.

Grandin also brought her research into play. Improving conditions for slaughtered animals, she argued, did not merely benefit the animals themselves. Grandin's research suggested that animals who were killed while calm produced better meat than those who died terrified. Better meat meant better prices for the companies and the ranchers. This economic argument was effective in convincing several slaughterhouses to switch to Grandin's designs.

Today

As of 2000, the restraint systems invented by Temple Grandin were increasingly the norm in the livestock industry. By one contemporary estimate, about a third of all cattle killed for the market were processed through Grandin-designed machines. During the same year, twenty of North America's thirty-two largest meatpackers used Grandin's systems; so did a number of hog and veal processors. Among her many other clients, Grandin advised McDonald's and the U.S. government on effective and humane slaughtering methods. "Slowly but surely her ideas are becoming a way of life,"[25] says the general manager of a meatpacking plant.

Today Grandin divides her time between her teaching job and her consulting business. She also lectures frequently. As the holder of a doctoral degree in animal science and the inventor of these new animal control systems, she is much in demand as a speaker among animal, scientific, and meat industry groups. As an autistic person whose career has been an enormous success, she has also been a popular lecturer on neurological issues. All in all, though some people might find it uncomfortable to design better systems for killing animals, Grandin is very pleased with her work and the career path she chose. "I've made a big difference with simple things," she says. "I enjoy designing equipment and getting people to do things right. That is satisfying."[26]

CHAPTER 2

Madame Walker

Being a successful inventor requires several important skills. First and perhaps most critical of all is imagination. At heart, most inventors are strong creative thinkers, people who enjoy attacking problems others find unsolvable and coming up with unexpected answers. The first step in any invention is theoretical: dreaming up a way to fill a need or fix a problem. The greatest and best-known inventions all began with a question. Robert Fulton's steamboat was an answer to the problem of how to get boats up a river quickly and easily; Thomas Edison's light bulb was a response to the need for a good way to produce more light indoors.

The second step in the invention process is to turn the dream into a reality. That step requires patience and ingenuity: building a model that will run, concocting a mixture that will work, finding a formula that will do the job. In some cases, the technical skills involved in this step are enormous. Orville and Wilbur Wright's invention of the airplane is one well-known example. The brothers devoted many months to the study of physics, aerodynamics, and mechanics; after many false starts, they drew on their knowledge and built a plane that could actually fly. In other cases, of course, the science is less complicated. Regardless of the degree of knowledge required, however, all inventors must put in the time and energy necessary to prove that their ideas are more than just theoretical.

Finally, a successful inventor must know something about marketing. Not all inventors do. The list of patent holders is dotted with names of people whose discoveries made life easier or more enjoyable—but who scarcely made a dime from their work. Many of these inventors are virtually unknown today. Unable or unwilling to get the word out about their inventions on their own, they sold their rights to others—who spent thousands of dollars to promote the inventions and made millions in sales. Countless other valuable inventions have languished unbought and unproduced, all because the inventor never spent any significant time trying to sell it. In the long run, inventors are only as wealthy as the strength of their marketing plan.

Dreaming, building, and selling: those are the steps of successful inventing, and Sarah Breedlove Walker was exceptionally good at all three. Known professionally as Madame—or Madam—C. J. Walker, she overcame an impoverished childhood and an unusually difficult adolescence to become what some have called the first African American woman millionaire. Walker produced an entire line of hair care products aimed at black women, and her marketing skills put those products in stores, homes, and beauty parlors

Sarah Walker became a millionaire by successfully creating and marketing hair care products for black women.

across America and several neighboring countries. Walker's standing in the African American community, too, was extremely high. In addition to being a clear success, both financially and socially, she was also a good role model.

Early Years

Madame Walker was born Sarah Breedlove on December 23, 1867. Her parents, Owen and Minerva Breedlove, had been slaves on a plantation near Delta, Louisiana, before the Civil War. With the coming of freedom at the end of the war, the Breedloves had opted to stay on and work white-owned land in exchange for a percentage of the crop. Called sharecropping, the system was not much of an improvement on slavery. As was usual in such arrangements, the Breedloves' hard work earned them very little money. Most of the proceeds, instead, went to the farmer who held the property. Thus, Madame Walker's family was constantly poor.

Matters quickly turned worse for young Sarah. Both her parents died when she was quite young. At the age of seven, Walker was taken in by an older sister, Louvenia, who moved with her from Louisiana to the nearby river town of Vicksburg, Mississippi. Louvenia, however, was married to an angry man who took out many of his frustrations on Walker. Years later, Walker remembered him as cruel, spiteful, and filled with contempt for her.

Finally, at the age of fourteen, Walker could stand it no longer. Determined to get out and unwilling to wait any longer to find a way, she took one of the few escape routes open to a young teenage girl of the time: marriage. In 1882 she married a man named Moses McWilliams. Within three years the couple had produced a daughter, whom they named Lelia (she would later call herself A'Lelia). Unfortunately, Moses McWilliams soon died, leaving Walker a nineteen-year-old widow with no job, no education, and a two-year-old to support.

It was necessary that Walker find a way to make a living, and quickly. She turned to the unskilled and laborious job of laundering. All day long Walker stooped over washboards and heavy iron tubs, cleaning and scrubbing clothes. Her hands wrinkled and her back usually ached. But few other options were available to her. An unschooled African American woman living in the South shortly after the Civil War was lucky to have a job at all.

Things did improve a few years later. Realizing that Louisiana and Mississippi were poor places to try to earn a living, Walker headed north to St. Louis, Missouri, in 1887. There, conditions were better for African Americans. Her earnings were higher, and

Using the savings from her laundering work, Walker was able to send her daughter, Lelia (pictured), to college in Tennessee.

she sent her daughter to the local public schools. After years of saving, Walker was even able to afford to send Lelia to a private college in Tennessee. St. Louis had a thriving black community, too, and was one of the leading centers of African American culture in the United States.

However, life was still difficult. Walker married again, this time to a man named John Davis, but the couple quickly divorced. Furthermore, being a laundress was taking a physical toll on Walker, and the money she made was not sufficient to allow for much beyond the education of her daughter and the basics of survival. From time to time she took on jobs as a domestic servant instead, but although these positions generally required less-intense work, they carried no more status and little, if any, extra pay. In addition, racism was common, even in a big city with a large African American population, and Walker's gender was a distinct handicap. As she looked around her, Walker recalled years later, she could not see how she would ever improve her condition.

Hair

The answer came from an unexpected source. By the time she was in her thirties, Walker had developed a somewhat embarrassing problem: Her hair was falling out. At the time, this was not an unusual complaint among African American women. The reasons varied. Poor diet was certainly one cause. Many of the women who suffered hair loss had little money and could not afford to eat well-balanced meals; thus, they missed out on certain nutrients necessary to maintain their hair. Another cause of hair loss was stress—never in short supply in the lives of early twentieth-century black women. And a third cause was complications resulting from other diseases and medical conditions.

Still, the biggest single cause of hair loss among African American women was probably the way most of them treated their hair. The stereotypical white beauty of the time had hair that was long and straight, and many black women tried to imitate this model. That was usually difficult. For the most part, African American hair did not lie straight—and it did not take easily to straightening. Nevertheless, having straight hair was seen as a mark of beauty, culture, and taste, and tightly curled hair was perceived as a reminder of the days of slavery. Thus, many African American women did their best to straighten their hair regardless of the difficulties.

Traditionally, African American women who wanted straightening began by dividing their hair into sections. Each section was wrapped with string and then twisted. When the hair was released and the twists combed out, the hair was indeed straighter. Unfortunately, there was a cost. The first, and most immediate, was discomfort. "You could hardly smile[,] it was so tight,"[27] recalls a woman who went through the process many times. Worse, women who used this process found that their hair soon tended to return to its natural curly state. As a result, they needed to repeat the process again and again. The more they twisted and tightened, the more they stressed their hair. Before too long, as in Walker's case, they found the strain too much for their scalp, and bare patches started to appear.

All was not lost, however. Because loss of hair was a problem for so many women, plenty of products were on the market that promised to restore and regrow what had been lost. These ranged from medicines for drinking to powders for rubbing on the affected spots. Even the names of the products offered hope: La Creole Hair Restorer and Thomas's Magic Hair Grower were just two of the myriad preparations available at the time. Unfortunately, the grand promises of the names rarely matched the restorative abilities of what was in the bottles. Some of the products were mildly effective, at least for a short time and for some of the women who used them. Most, however, were completely useless. At best, the women who bought them found that they were throwing their money away. More commonly, the medications contained ingredients that actually made the problem worse.

Desperate women, however, used any remedy they thought might help, and Madame Walker was no exception. Hoping to find something that would stop her hair loss, she went through one product after another. But nothing seemed to reverse her hair problems. In fact, the parade of pomades, ointments, and shampoos opened bald spots where they had not previously existed.

The Dream

At this point, according to Walker, God intervened. As she told the story years later, Walker prayed for help and received it in the form of a dream: "One night I had a dream, and in that dream a big black man appeared to me and told me what to mix up for my hair. Some of the remedy was grown in Africa, but I sent for it, mixed it, put it on my scalp, and in a few weeks my hair was coming in faster than it had ever fallen out."[28] The story of the dream is certainly romantic, and perhaps even partly true; only Madame Walker could tell for sure. However, the story leaves out Walker's persistence and determination. Although she may well have had a flash of sudden insight, Walker supplemented the dream with many experiments. Through intuition, observation, and trial and error she developed a formula that really did work.

Still, just because it worked for Madame Walker was no guarantee that the formula would be effective on other women. One by one, Walker approached her friends who also had troublesome hair. She offered them the chance to try her new product. Seeing what it had done for her made the decision easy for most; and, like Walker herself, most of these women were happy with the results. Sold on the formula's effectiveness, her friends urged her to market it on a larger scale. Walker, however, needed little encouragement: weary of domestic work, she was ready to try her hand at being in business for herself.

In July 1905 Walker took her first step: moving to Colorado, where some of her relatives lived. Arriving in Denver with only $1.50 in her pocket, Walker knew she would have to continue to work at other jobs before she could safely devote full time to her formulas. She ended up as a cook for a local pharmacist named E. L. Scholtz. It was a good match from Walker's perspective: evidence suggests that Scholtz used his chemistry background to help refine Walker's formula. Over the next few months, Walker used her free time to develop three hair care products, all of which seemed to be effective on her and her nieces. She called the products Wonderful Hair Grower, Vegetable Shampoo, and Glassine, and Walker decided to market them to the women of Denver.

Walker perfected her hair care solution with the aid of a pharmacist, and in 1905, she began marketing her product to the women of Denver, Colorado.

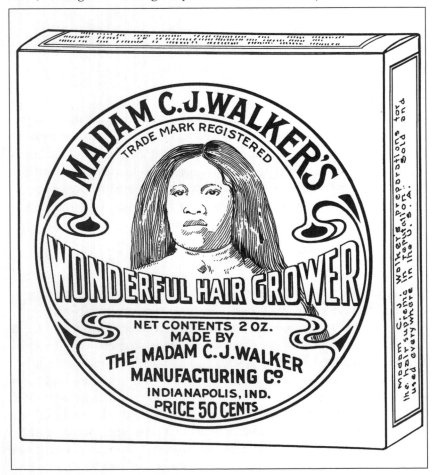

Advertising

Market them she did. Her game plan was clever and effective. Since Colorado had only a small African American population, Walker knew that finding appropriate hair products in mainstream stores was difficult. Thus, she targeted her sales pitch directly to the women themselves. Dressed neatly in a long skirt and a white blouse, Walker went door to door giving demonstrations. She shampooed her potential customers, medicated their scalps with her hair grower, and followed that up by styling their hair with a heated comb of Walker's own design. This initial treatment was free of charge, but Walker gambled that women who experienced it once would want to do so again.

She was right. Orders poured in. Women bought multiple bottles of Walker's products; better yet, they referred Walker to their friends. African American women had a long tradition of informal hairdressing, and in a small black community like Denver's, many women met in each other's homes to use Walker's products on each other. There was a political element to Walker's work as well. Invented, produced, and sold by a black woman, these products demonstrated that African American women could rely on themselves and on each other. "We's here to help one another," one of Walker's customers once stated, "and feel each other['s] care."[29]

Before long, word of Walker's products had expanded well beyond Denver. Although attracting business from other cities was wonderful, Walker soon found that filling orders from afar was a problem. To solve it, she turned to an old friend from St. Louis, a journalist named C. J. Walker. In 1906 he would become Madame Walker's third husband, but he first entered her business strictly as an adviser. C. J. had extensive experience in the mail-order business, and he helped establish systems for processing distant orders and making sure customers received them on time.

Together, the Walkers also began to advertise heavily. Black newspapers and black-oriented magazines, common in big cities, were obvious places for such ads, and the couple bought plenty of advertising space in these publications. Madame Walker's advertising copy was not at all modest. In accordance with the style of the time, Walker was fond of making grandiose claims and using such splashy slogans as "Supreme in Reputation" and "Once a User Always a User."[30] She also put her own picture on many of the advertisements. Sometimes Walker's picture appeared along with a picture of her before she began using her preparations. The contrast in hair health and general

First, Walker marketed her product door-to-door. Later, she expanded her strategy, placing advertisements like this one in popular black magazines and newspapers.

well-being was obvious; the comparison between the pictures no doubt helped convince many women to become new customers.

However, the cooperation between husband and wife did not last long. Soon the couple fell to arguing over the value of the business and Walker's expectations for it. "When we began to make ten dollars a day," Walker recalled years later, "he thought the amount was enough and I should be satisfied. But I was convinced that my hair preparations would fill a long-felt want, and when we found it impossible to agree, due to his narrowness of vision, I embarked on business for my-self."[31] The couple eventually divorced, but Madame Walker kept her new name and title. By this time, she was well known across the country. So, too, were her products.

Controversy

However, Walker's success involved controversy. Many African American thinkers worried that Walker's products bought into a distinctively white image of beauty. They preferred, instead, to play up the notion that thick, curly hair was both natural for black women and beautiful in and of itself. One black organization denounced Walker for urging women to style their hair according to what many members perceived to be white ideals.

Walker found particular opposition within African American churches. She had hoped to use them to spread the word about her products: then as now, churches were central meeting places within many African American communities. Most of the clergymen she approached, though, made it clear that they would not support her. "You should stay the way God made you," an old friend of Walker's recalled some ministers saying to her. "You're trying to straighten our hair and make us look white."[32]

Walker had a ready rebuttal to this charge. As she explained it, she did not "straighten" hair. Any straightening was incidental to her real goal, a goal that she believed the clergymen should have supported. Her purpose, she often explained, was to improve a woman's personal appearance by whatever means necessary. "I grow hair," she once told a reporter. "I want the great masses of my people to take a greater pride in their appearance and to give their hair proper attention."[33]

The clergymen did have a point. Even if straightening was not the purpose of her work, Walker was indeed encouraging black women to adopt an unnatural hairstyle that adhered to typical white standards of the time. Still, Walker was not the root of the problem. Prejudice in the early twentieth century was rampant. Denied the chance to see role models who resembled themselves, many African Americans did look to white society for social, political, and beauty cues. In helping women fulfill this desire, Walker was far from alone. Black-owned companies produced and marketed a range of beauty products that went well beyond any of Walker's in encouraging their customers to "think white." One business, for instance, sold a skin bleach called "Black No More."[34]

Nor was it fair to charge that Walker ignored the needs of her race. Walker's advertisements, in particular, showed a deep concern and empathy for the problems faced by African Americans. For example, Walker often appealed to buyers by looking to racial pride. "No greater force is working to glorify the womanhood of our Race than Madam C. J. Walker's Wonderful Hair and Skin Preparations,"[35] read a typical advertisement. Walker made it clear to her customers that she herself was black and had grown up in poverty, so she was well acquainted with the concerns of her customers.

Indeed, Walker also changed some of the traditions of advertising in African American newspapers. Before her time, most ads in these publications showed extremely light-skinned women whose features and skin tone were nearly white. By putting her own picture on her ads, Walker, a dark woman who would never have been mistaken for a Caucasian, broke the mold. To be sure, Walker used these pictures in hopes of economic gain. She believed that a beauty product was better off showing a woman who looked like her customers, who in turn could better imagine what effect the preparations would have on their own hair. Nevertheless, if Walker had indeed been completely absorbed by white ideals of beauty, it is reasonable to expect that she would have used a lighter model—or retouched the picture to make herself seem whiter. In fact, she did neither. Walker's use of herself as an advertising model helped pave the way for the flowering of a distinctively African American beauty culture.

On the Road

Madame Walker worked tirelessly to promote her product. Even when mail order and newspaper advertisements began to make up the bulk of her sales, she never forgot her roots. Her business had

While traveling and sightseeing throughout the United States, Walker gave demonstrations about her products and continued to connect with customers in a personal way.

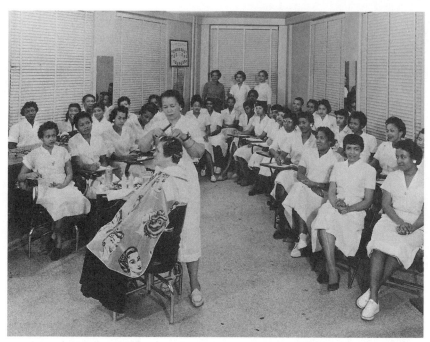

A Lelia College class pays close attention to the methods of hair care.

succeeded originally because of the personal touch: Her first sales had been made door-to-door to women in their homes. In 1906 she decided to renew this strategy of making connections. Noting the large population of African Americans in the South and the urban areas of the East and Midwest, Walker put the mail-order business in the hands of her daughter, now twenty-one, and left Denver. For the next two years, she traveled extensively, hoping to meet as many African American women as she could. Wherever she went, she gave demonstrations, taught her methods, and peddled her products. Again, the personal touch prevailed, and sales skyrocketed.

Even though business was booming, Walker was still far from satisfied. In 1908 she opened a branch office in Pittsburgh, a larger city than Denver at the time and one with a larger African American population. Two years later she moved again, this time transferring her base of operations to Indianapolis. That city's central location and extensive transportation network meant that shipping would be easier and cheaper from there than from almost anywhere else. Along the way she opened a beauty school called Lelia College, dedicated to teaching prospective black beauticians the basics of hair care. The school's curriculum became widely known as the Walker System—yet another way in which Madame Walker helped establish herself as a major figure in the beauty business.

A 1928 group photograph of Walker's agents. Madame Walker employed these individuals to promote and sell her hair care system.

Walker's personal magnetism also led to what was probably her most brilliant marketing strategy. Her travels had introduced her products to women throughout the country. More to the point, however, traveling had introduced Walker herself to women in many regions. Excited as they were by the products themselves, many of these women were even more impressed by Walker. Here was an unusual woman indeed—a black woman who had struck it rich, who was a clear success, yet who had not abandoned her people and her origins. It would have been understandable had Walker put on airs and sought to distance herself from her customers, but she did not. The combination of the formulas and Walker's personality meant that many of these women recommended the company's products to their friends with an almost missionary zeal. "I will be more than glad to recommend your remedies here to any of my color," a customer wrote to Walker in 1918, "as I feel so assured in them that they will do all you claim."[36]

Agents

Walker was delighted by the enthusiasm with which these women talked about her products. Each mention, after all, was worth a possible sale. As time went on Walker realized that she could make even better use of many of these women by hiring them as agents to promote her company. The women would do what Walker did on her tours: demonstrate, market, and promote her hair care system. In return, Walker paid her agents a base wage and a commission on the amount they sold.

The arrangement was beneficial to both parties. The agents, most of whom had been shut out of good jobs by prejudice, lack of skills, and poor education, were delighted to have the work. "You have opened up a trade for hundreds of colored women to make an honest and profitable living," an admirer wrote to her. "They make as much in one week as a month's salary would bring from any other position that a colored woman can secure."[37] Indeed, the women gained not only money but also valuable business experience. Moreover, with Walker's encouragement, they became leaders within their communities. They raised money for charitable causes and involved themselves in political issues of significance to blacks.

But Walker and her company benefited, too. The agents spread the word about the company's products, enabling Walker to cut back on her dizzying travel schedule. Furthermore, Walker saw that her products would sell best if recommended by women within her customers' communities. In her view, friends should be helping friends, sisters should be sharing what they knew about hair care, mothers should be passing down beauty tips to their daughters. Walker herself did not have that relationship with her customers, but most of her agents did. By adding the personal touch, Walker ensured high sales. The agent system is still used today by various companies, including Mary Kay cosmetics and Tupperware containers. In the early twentieth century, however, it was relatively new, and Madame Walker was among the first to popularize it.

Business, Charity, and Community

By 1911, soon after establishing the agent system, Madame Walker was virtually a household name among American blacks. Within the next few years her star rose ever higher. Walker's company became the country's dominant producer of beauty products for black women and one of the leading producers of beauty products for any race. Proceeds were so large that Walker became the first black American woman millionaire. She moved to Harlem, then to the suburbs of New York City, where she built a $250,000 estate with twenty rooms and a $60,000 pipe organ.

Walker did not let her success spoil her, however. Recognizing that her wealth and authority made her something of a role model, she decided to use her position for the good of society—and especially for the good of African Americans. She built a school in West Africa for the purpose of educating girls, then helped fund it. She spent large sums of money to encourage blacks to open businesses, and she spent even more to help support them through hard times. Her financial gifts to educational and political organizations promoting black culture and life were generous. She was noted especially for her support of antilynching groups, the National Association for the Advancement of Colored People, and the Colored YMCA of Indianapolis.

Just as Walker did not allow racism to push her down, neither did she allow sexism to destroy her. In 1912 she attended the convention of the National Negro Business League. The president of the organization, Booker T. Washington, refused to schedule a time for her to make a speech, but she was undaunted: On the last day of the convention, she got to her feet and addressed the delegates anyway. Her speech, both moving and inspirational, addressed the hardships she had faced and the determination with which she had overcome them:

> Surely you are not going to shut the door in my face. I feel that I am in a business that is a credit to the womanhood of our race. I am a woman who came from the cotton fields of the South. I was promoted from there to the washtub. Then I was promoted to the cook kitchen, and from there I promoted myself into the business of manufacturing hair goods and preparations. . . . I have built my own factory on my own ground.[38]

"Her Work Still Lives"

Madame Walker's hair care products represented a change from many of the other ones available to blacks of the time. Her formulas included sulfur, the so-called miracle ingredient that made her prod-

Lelia College's graduating class of 1934, Chicago, Illinois.

ucts distinctive. But by itself, the discovery was relatively unimportant. An invention is only as strong as its marketing plan, and marketing was what Walker did best. Her charismatic personality, her willingness to talk directly with people, and her total assurance that her product would work made up for any flaws in the formulas themselves. In the end, Walker's invention did not sell itself; instead, her personality, her forcefulness, and her agents sold it.

Similarly, although her invention did change the way women thought about their hair, Walker's tireless marketing and her example had effects that reached far beyond the question of hair or even of beauty. Walker showed African Americans that they could be successful, that they could overcome long odds, and that hard work and determination could lead them out of poverty. By hiring agents and giving donations to her community, too, Walker helped black women and men establish their own businesses, increase their level of service, and raise their sights higher than they might have otherwise. When she died in 1919, at the relatively young age of fifty-one, black educator Mary McLeod Bethune eulogized her as "the clearest demonstration I know of Negro woman's ability recorded in history. She has gone, but her work still lives and shall live as an inspiration to not only her race but the world."[39] Few people who knew her would have disagreed.

CHAPTER 3

Rose O'Neill

Rose Cecil O'Neill's invention was not the least bit practical. It involved no electric current and was based on no obvious mechanical principles. It did not lead to better communication, make the world a safer place to live, or save time and money for thousands of American families. She was no scientist and never called herself one, and although she did lay claim to being a humanitarian, her invention had little to do with her ventures in that area.

Yet O'Neill's invention was nevertheless an important part of early twentieth-century cultural history. Her success was due not to technical prowess but rather to creativity, intelligence, and the luck that went along with being in the right place at the right time. For children growing up in America around the time of the First World War, O'Neill's inventions were as familiar as Tickle Me Elmos, Cabbage Patch Kids, and Furbys were to later generations. Indeed, her inventions had much in common with these recent toys. A designer, author, and illustrator by trade, O'Neill was the inventor of the Kewpie (pronounced Q-P) doll—a fad that overtook the United States like few others before or since.

Beginnings

"The fairies endowed Rose O'Neill with dazzling gifts,"[40] a biographer once remarked, and some of these gifts were apparent early on. Born in Wilkes-Barre, Pennsylvania, on June 25, 1874, O'Neill grew up mainly in Omaha, Nebraska, where her parents encouraged her interests in drama, music, and art. At the age of fourteen she first came to public attention when she entered a contest for young artists run by a local newspaper. Her drawing, which she called *Temptation Leading Down into an Abyss,* won first place and a prize that O'Neill recalled at various times as being either five or ten dollars.

By all accounts, the picture was impressive. At first, the committee of judges doubted that the drawing had really been done by a child. It seemed to them too sophisticated to be the work of such a young person. When they were finally convinced that she was the artist, the newspaper editors hired her to do a weekly series of drawings. The money she earned was quite welcome to her family; her father had worked as a salesman and a book dealer, among several other jobs, but had never been a financial success.

Art was a clear talent for O'Neill, but it was not the only creative outlet she had. At the age of sixteen O'Neill briefly joined a traveling theater troupe. The experience did not suit her, however. The Shakespearean roles she was asked to play turned out to be more difficult than she had expected, so she returned to the visual arts and resolved to become a professional illustrator. Over the next year or two she churned out illustrations and sold them to magazines based in Chicago, Denver, and other cities.

A Move East

It was unusual enough for a teenage girl to be selling illustrations to magazines in nineteenth-century America, but what happened next was even rarer. When O'Neill was seventeen the rest of her family moved to Missouri. But O'Neill headed in another direction altogether. She went to New York City, where she lived at a Manhattan convent and enrolled in a few art classes. Before long, however, she dropped the classes to concentrate on marketing her illustrations.

New York was the hub of the publishing world, and the place where O'Neill was most likely to sell her drawings. She soon began selling illustrations to well-known New York magazines such as *Puck* and *Harper's Monthly.* As her reputation grew, she steadily expanded her client list until she was among the most popular of all magazine illustrators of the time. Soon she moved into advertisements as well; she became well known and respected for her drawings promoting Kellogg's Corn Flakes, Jell-O, and many other products still familiar today.

Editors appreciated her style even though she had

While still a teenager, Rose O'Neill began a career selling her illustrations such as this one to well-known New York City magazines.

two strikes against her. For one, she was a woman in a male-dominated field in an age when sexism was rampant. Consequently, for a time she signed her illustrations simply with her initials—RCO, for Rose Cecil O'Neill. Although editors were aware that she was a woman, the public was not. It would be some time before the truth would be widely known.

The other problem was that O'Neill's range was severely limited. In a sense, she had never truly learned to draw. In later life, she freely admitted as much: The few art lessons she had taken had done little to improve her technique or make her a more able artist. "She knows so little about perspective," a reporter once said about her, "that she is baffled by even so simple a feat as putting a table or chair into a picture for background."[41] Her editors, however, did not mind O'Neill's lack of technical skill. Instead, they appreciated her hard work, creative flair, attention to detail, and comical pictures that typically showed cute children, whimsical animals, and big-eyed fairies and similar creatures from her imagination.

Career and Personal Life

With or without technical skill, by the early 1900s O'Neill's career was taking off. The money she made from illustration allowed her to try her hand at other artistic projects as well. In 1904 she wrote a novel, which she called *The Loves of Edwry*. Two years later she spent time in Europe, where she dabbled in sculpture. She wrote poetry, too, and began to surround herself with other creative people. By all accounts, she relished the artistic lifestyle and loved to see herself as an unconventional free spirit.

Unfortunately, whereas O'Neill's career was going well, her personal life was not. In 1896 she married a businessman named Gray Latham. Latham took part in O'Neill's career, even appearing in some of her drawings as a model, but he seems to have been jealous of the money she made and anxious to control it. In any case, the marriage was not a happy one, and the couple divorced in 1901. O'Neill married again soon afterward, this time to a former magazine editor, Harry Leon Wilson. As had been true with Latham, Wilson also involved himself in his wife's work. He wrote two books that O'Neill illustrated, and he brought her further into the New York City literary world.

The marriage to Wilson, in the end, turned out to be no happier for O'Neill than the marriage to Latham had been. In part, the problem was a gap in personality. O'Neill was bright and bubbly, known for a rather wild sense of humor and a consuming interest in people, especially artistic ones. She saw herself as a great creative soul bound by no ordinary standards. As a result, O'Neill spoke frequently in baby talk; favored long, flowing robes; and made grand and passionate speeches about the meaning of art. Wilson, on the other hand, was sarcastic, moody, and often depressed. He was a poor match for his vibrant wife. In 1908 the couple separated; as she put it years later, she had "withdrawn from marriage,"[42] this time permanently.

Discouraged by two successive marital failures, O'Neill returned to Missouri to live with her family. Her earnings had helped them purchase an estate in

Following the end of her second marriage, O'Neill retreated to Bonniebrook, her Ozark estate.

the Ozarks, an estate that the family called Bonniebrook. Money was not a problem. O'Neill continued to illustrate and send her drawings to her editors through the mail. Though she missed the excitement and the literary world of New York, she suspected she needed time away.

The Kewpies

Apparently time away was exactly what she needed, for in 1909 O'Neill made the drawings that would eventually make her famous. Her artistic style had been veering more and more toward the cute and sentimental, and she sent off a few illustrations that included several round, cherubic babies with big eyes, tiny wings, and fat cheeks.

Exactly where O'Neill got the idea for these creatures is open to some debate. According to one version, she modeled them on a pug-nosed dog given to her by a friend. According to another, attributed to O'Neill herself, the creatures came to her in a dream. According to still a third version, reported on a different occasion by O'Neill, they were a very deliberate cross between Cupid, the Roman god of love, and her recollection of her youngest brother as a baby.

Whatever their origin, a magazine editor named Edward Bok was taken with their looks. He suggested that O'Neill use these figures as the basis for a short comic piece that would involve both writing and art. O'Neill readily agreed and drew up a number of these funny little creatures. Distinctively her creation, they were drawn complete with oversize heads, topknots, and tiny wings. Determining a name was easy, she said: Each was to be called a Kewpie. "Kewpie means a small Cupid," she explained to her readers, "just as puppy means a small dog."[43]

However, O'Neill was quick to add that the Kewpies were quite different from Cupid. "Cupid gets himself into trouble," she remarked. "The Kewpies get themselves out, always searching out ways to make the world better and funnier."[44] There would be dozens of Kewpies, she decided, and their world would be one of mild disaster, gentle humor, and fun. She strove to bring out the endearing physical characteristics of babies in her drawings of the Kewpies (or Kewps, as she called them for short) while playing up the mischief they made and their essential goodness in the text.

In December 1909 the first Kewpie story appeared in the *Ladies' Home Journal,* Edward Bok's magazine. Entitled "The Kewpies' Christmas Frolic," the tale set the tone for the ones that would follow. O'Neill tells about the Kewpies' lives in what one critic has called "quite excruciating verse,"[45] of which this four-line excerpt is typical:

> The Kewpie wights stay up at nights,
> All gayly singing rum-te-tum,
> Like puddings they are pleasant sights,
> Well rounded at the tum-te-tum.[46]

After setting the scene, O'Neill developed the plot. The Kewpies were planning to spend their Christmas Eve playing practical jokes on people by leaving them inappropriate presents: guns for grandmothers, dictionaries for babies. However, their playfulness turned to sorrow when they saw a poor girl who would receive no presents at all, and they spent the remainder of the evening transferring gifts to her house from the home of Gwendolyn Van Schuyler Peeps, a rich girl. In the place of Gwendolyn's presents, O'Neill writes, one Kewpie burrowed into her Christmas stocking:

> Lucky, lucky Gwendolyn!
> The only, only, only one
> Is Gwendolyn Van Schuyler Peeps
> That ever had a Kewp for keeps.[47]

But if the verse was unmemorable, the same could not be said of the pictures. O'Neill, by now writing under her full name, illustrated the poem with two crowd scenes showing about a dozen Kewpies each. In the first drawing, the creatures gazed sadly on the poor girl asleep in her empty bedroom; in the second, they smiled as they moved the presents out of Gwendolyn's room. Although the reader's eye was drawn to those two scenes, O'Neill also arranged several smaller pictures on the page. In each case, O'Neill managed to draw the Kewpies with both whimsy and emotion. The characters were cute without being overly romanticized; at the same time, they looked similar enough to real toddlers to strike a responsive chord in the reader.

Success

"The Kewpies' Christmas Frolic" was soon followed by other Kewpie adventures—"The Kewpies and the Baby," "The Kewpies and the Aeroplane," and many more. As the *Ladies' Home Journal* series developed, its popularity soared. Other magazine editors clamored for Kewpie stories of their own. Readers snapped up the publications in which the creatures appeared. O'Neill quickly issued a Kewpie children's book, hoping to capitalize on the increasing mania for all things Kewpie before the fad died out.

She need not have worried. The Kewpie craze only grew. Two more Kewpie books appeared, and demand among magazines for the cartoony figures continued to soar. O'Neill marketed and sold paper dolls, called Kewpie Kutouts, based on the stories, and still interest rose. Kewpie soap appeared in stores; so did Kewpie saltshakers, Kewpie handkerchiefs, and more, all licensed by O'Neill herself. Delighted and more than a little bit surprised, O'Neill watched as money and notoriety rolled in.

The fad was still growing strong in 1912, three years after the initial Kewpie story

The Kewpies appeared in a series of stories in the Ladies' Home Journal. As their popularity increased, so did the demand for anything Kewpie.

had appeared, and O'Neill decided to take advantage of the excitement by marketing something new: a line of Kewpie dolls. With the help of a design student at Pratt Institute in New York City, she created a prototype and offered it to a local toy company. The company jumped at the chance. Quickly, O'Neill patented her design, thus giving her financial and creative control over the dolls. Gwendolyn Van Schuyler Peeps, back in the first Kewpie story, may have once been the "only one . . . who ever had a Kewp for keeps,"[48] but if O'Neill had her way, that would no longer be true. Instead, Kewps would be available in doll form to everyone.

Dolls

O'Neill's idea was nothing new. The idea of making a toy representation of a human figure is older than recorded history: Dolls of clay and stone have been found in archaeological sites dating back several millennia. It is difficult to tell today how many of these dolls were intended for children's use. Some were no doubt earmarked for other functions instead: They may have been fertility symbols, for example, or used as part of a funeral rite. Still, many experts believe that at least some of these early figurines were used as toys. "As in primitive tribes of today the children will create a simple image from sticks or even from a daubed stone," writes one doll expert, "so the child in the dawn of history would have found the need for some simple object to share his existence."[49]

Certainly, there is ample evidence that dolls were popular among children of early civilizations. The Egyptians made dolls from wood, linen, and papyrus leaves, some of which have survived more or less intact for nearly four thousand years. The ancient Greek historian Plutarch wrote of his two-year-old daughter's fondness for a doll—and her request for more to play with. Likewise, doll-making was an important business in the Roman Empire, with craftspeople turning out not merely dolls but also accessories designed to be used with them such as face paint, clothing, and even jewelry.

But doll making really took off as an industry in nineteenth-century Europe. The specimens most highly sought after by doll collectors date from this period. In Germany, France, England, and other countries, workers began to manufacture dolls in quantity, combining the care and traditions of an old craft with the new ideas of mass production. In earlier years manufactured dolls were only for wealthy children. The poor (and often the middle class as well) used whatever materials were on hand to stitch together and stuff a makeshift doll of their own.

A Japanese woman holds a Kewpie doll. By the early twentieth century, the dolls became popular children's toys and were mass produced.

But the nineteenth century changed that. As the number of dolls produced went up, the price went down. Further, new methods of manufacture and new materials made it possible to increase production and lower prices still more. In particular, whereas earlier dolls intended for commercial sale had typically been carved from wood, made from china, or molded from plaster, papier-mâché, or wax, the nineteenth century saw a new innovation called bisque.

The word *bisque* was related to *biscuit,* which in this case referred to a method of making unglazed porcelain. Compared to other materials, working with bisque was easy and cheap, and manufacturers flocked to produce bisque dolls. Some of these dolls sold for very little money indeed. For the first time, doll makers set their sights not only on attracting the attention of well-off children but also on selling to those of much more modest means.

A Smashing Success

Rose O'Neill's plan to market dolls, then, came along at a good time. The early years of the twentieth century were excellent ones for doll makers. The market was large and still growing; all but the very poorest families could afford a doll or two for their children. Aiming for the broadest possible market, O'Neill chose to

The first Kewpie dolls were made out of bisque and looked just like the characters in O'Neill's stories.

manufacture the first Kewpies in bisque. In 1912 she headed to a German doll factory to oversee the production of the earliest Kewpie examples.

The response was overwhelming. The dolls were reasonably well made, and they looked just like the Kewpies in the magazines, down to the bemused expressions and the slightly unkempt topknots. Americans were eager to own them, and the first run of dolls sold out almost immediately. The toy company ordered a second run, then a third. Each of these sold out as well. Realizing that her invention had struck a nerve, O'Neill and the toy company owners decided to branch out. If the people wanted Kewpies, they reasoned, then they would give the public what it wanted.

And so an astonishing variety of Kewpie dolls hit the market in the next several years. Most of these, like the earliest examples, were made out of bisque. However, the company also produced dolls made from other materials, including celluloid, wood, ivory, and even rubber. Kewpies appeared in all manner of sizes, from tiny two-inch models easy enough to stuff into a purse or pocket all the way up to toys half the size of the preschoolers who lugged them around wherever they went. O'Neill knew she was creating dolls to fit every budget and taste. She instructed her workers to handle the littlest dolls with the same care and concern they gave the bigger ones; as she once was quoted as saying, the smallest dolls "were for the poorest children."[50]

Size and material were not the only variations. Although only a few of the Kewpies had been given names and personalities in the original stories, O'Neill quickly issued a number of individual character dolls. People could buy "Carpenter," "Cook," "Careful of His Voice," and several others, just as customers today have a seemingly endless line of Barbie figures or action toys from which to choose. O'Neill also issued a few Kewpies in pairs, showing them involved in social activities such as reading or hugging; she called these "Instructive Kewpies."[51]

Still, the most popular Kewpies were the basic models, which O'Neill called "plain." These were medium-sized, with no frills. Unlike some of the more ornate models O'Neill produced, these dolls were sold without costumes and had painted eyes rather than glass ones. These plain Kewpies were beloved by the carnival industry, which bought thousands to give away as prizes. Long after Kewpies had reached their height of popularity, they were still common giveaway items, and many young men tried their best to win Kewpie dolls for their girlfriends at county fairs and midways across the country.

But carnivals were far from the only market for Kewpie dolls. Although Kewpie soap, Kewpie books, and all other Kewpie items had been tremendously popular, they were no match for the dolls. Kewpie mania spread across the nation. Kewpie clubs formed to trade the dolls and to talk about them. Children begged their parents for the toys. People bought them to use as party favors and as cake decorations. Along with her sister Callista, O'Neill opened a Kewpie store in Manhattan.

Years went by, and the market showed no signs of collapsing. In 1914, however, Kewpie mania was dealt a potentially harsh blow by the outbreak of World War I. Though the United States would not join the war for nearly three years, the war nevertheless disrupted the manufacture of the Kewpies. Worse, since Germany was considered the aggressor in the war, several countries cut off shipments of German-produced goods, although, according to some sources, England made a temporary exception for Kewpie dolls. Worried about the situation and concerned that the United States

Kewpie dolls were popular prizes at carnivals and fairs long after the fad peaked.

might enter the war against Germany, O'Neill and her partners moved operations to the United States shortly after the war began. And still children clamored for Kewpies.

Afterward

By the early 1920s the fad finally died down, and the public moved on to other diversions. Rose O'Neill, though, had made out extremely well. In all, she earned an estimated $1.5 million from the Kewpies, much of it from the sale and manufacture of the various Kewpie dolls. Her invention had paid off handsomely.

Although she kept working, O'Neill never achieved anything quite so lucrative or popular again. In 1925 she tried to market a similar doll, a more realistic follow-up to the Kewpies, called "Scootles." It was not a success. She also continued to illustrate, but her Kewpie earnings allowed her to take on only projects that truly interested her, and she did less and less as time went on. Turning more to writing, she published three more novels and a book of serious poetry. All got mixed reviews. Critics praised the "sheer beauty of [her] expression"[52] and used words such as *enchanting* and *whimsical* to describe the best of her work. However, many reviewers also found that her work was sometimes too much of a good thing. One critic complained about her "dangerous tendency toward . . . large romantic gestures" and "a cloying touch of whimsy."[53]

But O'Neill cared little about what the critics thought. She was wealthy, and she worked hard to project herself as a brilliant, creative thinker whose feelings and ideas were all beyond those of most people. She split her time between Bonniebrook and a mansion in Connecticut conveniently close to Manhattan. The former, she felt, was "a good place to unbutton,"[54] but the excitement of the New York literary scene was undeniable.

O'Neill surrounded herself with young artists and writers and supported them with time, words of encouragement, and money. Her Connecticut house became a colony for creative people. O'Neill paid for meals, housing, and elaborate gifts. Few of these visitors ever amounted to much in the creative world, but that did not matter to O'Neill, who was determined to work hard to promote their work regardless. "They were all geniuses to her," reported a journalist who visited O'Neill later in her life, "for it was by their intentions and not by their works that she judged them."[55] One couple, invited to spend a weekend with her, wound up staying for two years, and those who knew her well insisted that this was not an isolated event.

During the remainder of her post-Kewpie life, O'Neill continued to be viewed as a rather eccentric genius. Some emphasized the genius part. "There is something stupendous about Rose

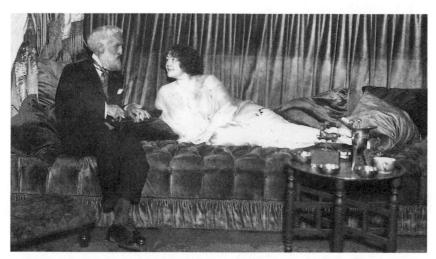

O'Neill entertained many artists and writers in her Connecticut home, giving them encouragement and often bestowing lavish gifts upon them.

O'Neill," remarked a newspaper writer in 1922. "She is not to be judged by any of our ordinary standards [but] belong[s] to that small band to whom we willingly accord the title of Master."[56] Others played up the eccentricities. O'Neill, for example, was given to walking barefoot and continued her habit of wearing striking red robes whenever possible. She called her Connecticut home Carabas Castle after the castle in the fairy tale "Puss in Boots." And in a nod to the invention that made it all possible, she gave a name to her hot water heater as well: Kewpio.

Unfortunately, even the earnings from the Kewpies were not enough to keep O'Neill in this kind of life forever. Years of lavish entertaining, extreme generosity, and a willingness to spend all kinds of money on her home gradually depleted her fortune. In 1936 she gave up Carabas Castle and returned permanently to Bonniebrook. There, she tried one last time to repeat her success with Kewpies by inventing and marketing another doll, this one a small Buddha-like figure she called Ho-Ho. Again, her attempt was a failure, and she died almost penniless near Bonniebrook in 1944.

Today, however, O'Neill has not been forgotten. Her invention of the Kewpie doll sparked one of the greatest fads of the twentieth century. Kewpies are still part of popular culture: Collectors seek them out, and many later dolls have been modeled at least partly on their looks. O'Neill did it all with little scientific background but quite a good deal of intelligence, luck, and creativity. "Do good deeds in a funny way," she liked to say. "The world needs to laugh or at least smile more than it does."[57] In every aspect of her life, Rose O'Neill embodied this philosophy.

CHAPTER 4

Grace Hopper

Today it is difficult to travel far in the United States without encountering a computer. Machines and gadgets ranging from cars on down to hand-held video games often contain built-in computing devices. Banks, supermarkets, and corporations rely on computers to store and process transactions. Full-size personal and business computers can be found in libraries, schools, offices, and homes.

Those who have access to these machines appreciate these computers' capabilities. Word processing, spreadsheets, Internet connections, games—all are readily available on even the smallest computers for sale today. Americans increasingly take it for granted that they will have access to a quick, small, and powerful computer for work and for pleasure.

But this was not always the case. The pace of technological change has been remarkably swift, and computers are comparatively quite new. The memories of many living people today go back long before any viable computer existed. And even when computers had actually been built, most people found them simply a curiosity. Few people used them daily. Programming them was an extremely complex task, and compared to modern-day versions, early computers were slow, enormous, and extraordinarily expensive. As a result, only a few government offices and large corporations actually owned computers.

Many changes helped bring computers into the center of public life. Some of these were cultural, but most were technological. With each new innovation, scientists increased computers' storage capabilities, sped up the time computers needed to process information, and simplified programming methods. To go from the ponderous mainframes of World War II to the sleek and efficient personal computers on desks at the beginning of the twenty-first century, many engineers and scientists played important roles. But among the most important of these men and women was a naval commander, mathematician, and inventor named Grace Hopper.

Growing Up

Grace Hopper was born Grace Murray on December 9, 1906, in New York City. The years surrounding her birth were a time of rapid changes in technology. The telephone, invented a few years earlier by Alexander Graham Bell, was beginning to change the way people communicated with one another. The automobile, another relatively recent invention, was likewise altering people's ideas of transportation. So did the airplane: The Wright brothers had made their first successful flight at Kitty Hawk, North Carolina, just three years earlier.

Like all American children of the period, Hopper was well aware of these inventions as she grew up. Hopper's family, however, placed special value on technological progress. As a result, Hopper learned more about the importance of these inventions than the average child of the time. Both of her grandfathers had been involved in engineering and contracting—businesses that required plenty of mathematics and science. Hopper was encouraged to follow up her interests in these areas. Years later, Hopper recalled going on surveying projects with one grandfather, even holding the surveyor's pole for him while he took measurements—a very unusual chore for a girl in the early twentieth century.

As a young girl, Hopper also spent a lot of time examining how things worked. "I built everything," she says. "Ships, railroad cars, bridges, even furniture for my sister's dollhouse."[58] Few girls of the time were encouraged to build, but Hopper's parents believed that technical know-how was as important for their daughters as it was for their sons. Sometimes, though, even the Murrays felt that young Grace went too far. At the age of seven, for example, Hopper became consumed by the question of how alarm clocks worked. To find out, she took hers apart. Unable to put it back together again and still unsure what made it run, she proceeded to take apart all of the other clocks she could find in the house—six more altogether—before finally being stopped by her mother. The incident was typical of Hopper's early years.

Hopper did well through elementary and high school. Science and mathematics came especially easy to her. She liked geometry best because, as she remembered years later, "When I did geometry problems, I could use all the colored pencils."[59] Following high school graduation in 1924, she attended Vassar College in Poughkeepsie, New York, where she majored in mathematics and physics. She also took as many other science courses as possible. Not satisfied yet, Hopper moved on to Yale University in New Haven, Connecticut where she earned a master's degree in math in 1930. She also met and married her husband, college professor Vincent Hopper; the couple, however, would divorce in 1945.

Professor and Lieutenant

Grace Hopper's first years after earning her master's degree could have been extremely difficult. The Great Depression was in full swing, and jobs of any kind were scarce. That was especially true for women in the sciences. For years a strong prejudice had existed against women in technical fields. These were often considered by men and women alike to be men's specialties, and a woman with an interest in technology or numbers was viewed with suspicion. The depression exacerbated this problem. Employers were anxious to give jobs to men, especially those with wives and children, since they were considered the ones in charge of supporting their families. Most people did not feel that women needed jobs at all.

Hopper was lucky, however. In 1931 Vassar asked her to return as a professor of mathematics. She taught courses in topics ranging from statistics to calculus. By all accounts, Hopper was a well-respected teacher and an outstanding scholar. While employed at Vassar she found time to earn a doctoral degree in mathematics, a very unusual achievement for a woman of the time. She might have stayed the rest of her professional career at Vassar, but in 1941 the Japanese government bombed Pearl Harbor and the United States joined World War II.

World War II changed Grace Hopper's life forever. As the war dragged on, Hopper saw people all around her making new plans and moving in new and unexpected directions. Some of her relatives took jobs in the factories that produced ships, guns, and other war materials. Some of her students joined various branches of the military. Desperate to make a difference in the war effort herself, Hopper took a leave of absence from her teaching position and joined the U.S. Naval Reserve in December 1943. In 1944 she was commissioned a lieutenant.

Being a lieutenant in the naval reserves, though, did not necessarily mean that Hopper would spend her time aboard ships. In fact, Hopper did not. Then, as now, the navy needed not only sailors, commanders, and mechanics but also many thousands of support personnel: people to plan the routes ships would take, people to design the weapons the ships would carry, people to oversee the construction and deployment of the vessels. By the time she was made a lieutenant, naval officials already had a task in mind for Hopper—a task that perfectly fit her skills.

For several years the navy had been working on an important and mainly secretive computing project. The advantages of a computer were clear to many naval officials. Warfare is full of mathematical problems: At what angle should a gun be set in order to be most likely to hit its target? What is the most efficient way to move fifty thousand soldiers from one location to another, making sure not to waste fuel and food? How should bombs be placed on the seafloor to best interfere with enemy warships? A computer can answer these questions much more accurately, quickly, and efficiently than any mathematician can do by hand.

However, a truly effective computer was not yet a reality in 1943. A team of researchers at Harvard University in Boston, Massachusetts, had made some progress in building one for the navy, but it needed to do more research to make its creation truly workable. Hopper's math and science background, naval officials reasoned, made her a natural fit for the project. The fact that she knew nothing whatsoever about the still-young field of computer

Grace Hopper works on an early computer. Hopper's intelligence and curiosity made her the perfect candidate for the navy's computer project.

science did not deter them; her intelligence, scientific training, and curiosity would be enough to guarantee her success. As a result, Hopper went to Boston to begin work on the project.

Computers

The idea of a computer was not especially new. Early in the nineteenth century an English engineer named Charles Babbage had come up with a theoretical model of a machine that could perform complex calculations. Called an analytical engine, Babbage's idea was revolutionary. He imagined a machine divided into two parts: the "store," where numbers were kept as the machine worked on calculations, and the "mill," the part that actually performed the computations. Building such a computer, he wrote at the time, would spare people "the intolerable labor and fatiguing monotony"[60] of calculating everything by hand.

Babbage's machine might have been successful had the technology of the time supported his theories. Unfortunately, Babbage's era had only a dim understanding of the uses of electricity, and machine technology was poor in comparison to today. Thus, machines simply could not be built to the specifications that Babbage's project demanded.

In the early nineteenth century, George Babbage, an English engineer, tried to develop an analytical machine that could perform complex mathematical calculations.

Babbage spent thousands of dollars from his personal fortune, hoping that such a machine could be constructed, but he was doomed to failure. Today he is remembered not for inventing the computer but rather for his work examining what such a machine would be capable of doing and how it would go about carrying out its tasks.

Babbage was not the only nineteenth-century person to explore the concept of an analytical engine. Another important person in the history of the computer was Ada Lovelace, a friend of Babbage's and a brilliant mathematician herself. Lovelace's contribution was to invent a way of telling the machine what to do. Her solution was

Ada Lovelace invented and used punch cards as a way of feeding information to the analytical machine.

a series of punched cards, each of which—when fed into the machine— would provide it with a piece of information it needed to do its job. This idea had been adapted from the Jacquard weaving loom, in which holes in cards automatically adjusted the threads on the loom to form a weaving pattern. "We may say most aptly that the Analytical Engine weaves algebraical patterns just as the Jacquard loom weaves flowers and trees,"[61] Lovelace wrote in 1843.

Lovelace also made another important realization: The computer was not as smart as it appeared. Even if an analytical engine could actually be constructed, she argued, it would not be inherently intelligent. Rather, it would only be as smart as the instructions it was given and the person who operated it. "The Analytical Engine has no pretensions whatever to originate anything," she wrote in 1843. "It can do whatever we know how to order it to perform. It can follow analysis; but it has no power to anticipat[e] any analytical relationships or truths."[62] Whereas Babbage has been remembered as the developer of the computer, at least in spirit, Lovelace is considered today as the world's first programmer.

The Mark I

Babbage and Lovelace were ahead of their time, and interest in their work was relatively low for many years after their deaths. By the late 1930s, though, things had changed. Improvements in technology had made the computer a real possibility. In 1937 Harvard professor Howard Aiken produced a paper explaining how such a machine might be built. Soon Aiken was talking with Thomas Watson, the head of the technology company IBM. Together with a few other scientists and researchers, Aiken and Watson designed what was to become the Mark I computer. Built at a laboratory in Endicott, New York, the Mark I was moved to Harvard in 1944 and was immediately leased to the navy. This was, of course, the same year that Grace Hopper became a lieutenant.

The Mark I was "an impressive beast," Hopper recalled many years later. "She was fifty-one feet long, eight feet high, and five feet deep."[63] Behind a solid front, the computer consisted of several hundred miles of wire linked by mechanical switches. With some switches turned off and others on, electric current flowed across one sequence of wires; changing the switch settings sent the current flowing in different directions.

The switches opened and shut while the machine calculated. Each electrical impulse stood for a new number or commanded the machine to perform an operation on the number already read.

The first known computer, called the Mark I (pictured) was designed by Howard Aiken and Thomas Watson.

The constant clanking of the switches made the room in which the Mark I was stored sound just like a set of typewriters. There were no keyboards, monitors, or mouselike devices. "No one looking at it today," Hopper later said, "would really believe it was a computer. You'd hardly believe it was a calculator. . . . It would be hard to recognize Mark [I] in today's world."[64]

The electricity and the switches helped make the Mark I a useful machine. But what made it a computer was the fact that it could be programmed. A scientist could feed the computer a set of steps to perform, which the computer would then carry out automatically. As long as the steps made sense and did what the programmer wanted them to do, the computer would always find the proper answer. The Mark I was programmed through a series of punched holes similar to those devised by Ada Lovelace many years earlier. Punches on a long strip of tape sent codes to the machine. Each line on the tape stood for a new command. Essentially, the punches told the switches which way to move, and the positions of the switches specified the numbers used to calculate.

Hopper's new job was to learn programming, and to do it as quickly as possible. She would become just the third person to program the Mark I. Programming was exacting, careful work that required a logical and orderly mind, along with strong spatial and numerical skills. Although she had never programmed—or coded, to use the more common term of the time—a computer before, Hopper immersed herself into the world of computers. She studied the works of Babbage and Lovelace. She got help from two young naval men with some previous experience on the Mark I, and she asked frequent questions of other experts in the still-young field of computer science.

Hopper learned quickly. Within a few months she was assigned to write a programming manual for the Mark I. She objected strenuously, arguing that she could not write well and did not know enough about the subject. Her superior officer, however, was unsympathetic. The result, before long, was *The Manual of Operation for the Automatic Sequence Controlled Calculator.*

A New Model

For its time, the Mark I was formidable. In just one second it could carry out three addition problems—a rate much faster than a human calculator, no matter how skilled. Better yet, the machine never tired, and its mechanical parts could always be replaced as they wore out. Even at this early stage, it was clear that the computer had a lot to offer the navy. Soon after Hopper started working on the Mark I, naval officials commissioned the building of a similar model, the Mark II, also at Harvard.

Mark I and Mark II had their share of problems, however. For one thing, the computers were not as durable as they needed to be. Mechanical problems were frequent. Switches broke. Wires snapped. Heat played havoc with the system. Once Hopper and her fellow programmers found that a moth had gotten into the workings of the Mark II. She stuck the insect into the day's logbook with the notation, "First actual bug found."[65] Some linguists trace the popularity of the computer phrase *a bug in the system,* meaning a problem in the works, to this discovery.

Nor were the computers as fast as the navy would have liked. Three calculations per second may sound speedy indeed, but in fact officials had so many questions to ask—and so many complex calculations to make—that the programmers could not keep up with the demand. An especially long set of computations might take several hours. Even though this was a far cry from the months it might have taken a human, it was still too slow for the needs of the navy. Along with keeping the machines in good mechanical order, Hopper and other mathematicians labored constantly to find a way to speed up the process.

But most serious of all, the two computers were not as accurate as naval commanders wished. The problem lay not in the wiring but rather in the programming process. Written language had to be turned into punched holes, and often the person doing the punching was not the person who had written the lines of code. Sometimes the punchers read letters or numbers incorrectly—a 9 might come out as a *4,* say. Other times a tired programmer might inaccurately write down the digits or might mix up the steps. Either way, the answer would be nonsense. If naval officials were lucky, it would immediately be clear that the answer was wrong. If they were unlucky, the answer looked right and was assumed to be so—leading to trouble in future calculations, potentially even a ship that could not float or a gun affixed incorrectly to the deck of a vessel.

Another complication was that these early programs were written one by one as the need arose. At first, no one had the time or the desire to make a list of useful programs that had already been written. However, as the number of programs increased, Hopper realized that a list would ultimately save time, not waste it. If two different programs both included the same mathematical computation, she reasoned, it made little sense to rewrite the steps for the computation from scratch. It would be much more reasonable to write a special program called a subroutine. This subroutine would list the steps necessary to make the computation. The programmer would check and double check the subroutine for accuracy, then insert it into the appropriate section of each larger program.

Hopper and her colleagues began to write and collect accurate subroutines. As she describes the process, "We had notebooks, and we had a piece of code that we had already checked out. . . . We would [then just] borrow each other's code that was already written. . . . And we would copy them in the new programs."[66] Hopper's idea proved well worth the time it took to write and test these miniprograms. Not only did inserting subroutines increase accuracy, it also sped up the process of writing programs.

After the War

World War II ended in 1945, bringing to a halt some of the work on Hopper's computer project. With the end of the war, Hopper had to decide what to do next. She had two offers: return to Vassar as a full professor of mathematics or remain at Harvard and carry on further research with the Mark I and the Mark II. As it happened, having to make a choice put Hopper squarely in the center of a rising debate about the value of computers.

There was little argument about the usefulness of the Mark I and the Mark II in helping to win the war. Most observers agreed that they had saved time, money, and effort. However, plenty of debate raged about the future of computers and computing. Many people believed that the value of computers had reached its peak. The machines' use outside wartime would be severely limited: Businesses, colleges, and other organizations would find them too bulky, too expensive, and too complicated to operate. Moreover, these critics argued, the Mark I and the Mark II, along with a few other computers being built at the time, would supply all of the computing needs for the world over the foreseeable future. Computers, in this scenario, would prove a dead end, and many people believed that Hopper would be well advised to return to academia.

For Hopper, however, the choice was clear. She had become captivated by what she was doing at Harvard and wanted to continue. Moreover, she predicted a rosy future for computers. In her mind, computers would prove every bit as valuable outside the navy as inside it. To her, the critics of computers were motivated not by careful analysis but by stubbornness and lack of imagination. Their opposition was based on the fact that, as she puts it, "we've never done it that way before"[67]—an attitude she never understood. Ignoring the critics, she stayed on.

Over the next few years Hopper worked on several computers, notably the Mark III, the Mark IV, and a machine called the Binary

Automatic Computer (BINAC). In the early 1950s she began work on another new computer, this one known as the Universal Automatic Computer (UNIVAC). During the six or seven years since Hopper had learned to program the Mark I, technology had improved considerably. UNIVAC was much smaller than the Mark I—just fourteen feet long and less than eight feet high. It calculated much more swiftly than the Marks, and the bulky punch system of programming had been discarded in favor of a magnetic tape.

Indeed, so many improvements had been made to the machine that UNIVAC's designers hoped to market their creation to the public. For the first time, many models of a computer would be produced and offered for sale. The computer would still be expensive enough that only the wealthiest businesses and institutions could afford it. Nonetheless, the pace of technology had been so quick that mass production had become a reasonable dream. UNIVAC's builders, a company called Remington Rand (later purchased by Sperry), took steps to make this dream a reality.

Unfortunately, even after all of the technical improvements one major problem remained: programming. Highly mathematical and still quite time-consuming to write and apply, the codes used by UNIVAC were gibberish to anyone not trained in mathematics. Worse, writing new codes—which would need to be done for each new software package—was a long and tedious task. Remington Rand officials realized that the complexity of the programming was a major deterrent to people interested in buying the computer.

The Compiler

The solution, however, was far from obvious, and company officials went down several dead ends in their attempts. At last Hopper suggested a revolutionary new idea based partly on her earlier work with subroutines. She proposed an entirely new kind of program called a compiler. The compiler had two major functions—functions that may appear obvious now but were not at all obvious in Hopper's time.

First, the compiler would translate the programming language into another, simpler code that the machine could easily read. The programming language used by UNIVAC's designers, for example, required that numbers be written in a system called octal, which relies on a base of eight rather than the base ten of our standard decimal notation. Major differences exist between the two systems. Whereas the base ten system uses the digits 0 through 9, base eight uses only 0 through 7. Likewise, place value in base ten is determined by powers of ten. A three-digit number indicates hundreds, tens, and

Based on the notion that repeated steps are unnecessary, Hopper designed the compiler (shown) which could translate computer languages and instruct the computer to program itself.

ones, with each place representing ten times the one to its immediate right. Thus, the number *237* is read as "two hundreds, three tens, and seven remaining." But in octal, place value relies on powers of eight: sixty-fours, eights, and ones, for a three-digit number. In this notation, *237* would refer to "two sixty-fours, three eights, and seven remaining," or the number *159* in base ten.

Learning base eight was a tricky process, even for an experienced mathematician like Hopper. A comedian once remarked, "Base eight is just like base ten really—if you're missing two fingers."[68] Hopper would no doubt have agreed with this rather wry sentiment. Though she quickly became proficient in performing operations in octal, she sometimes forgot to revert to base ten in her normal life: at one point her checkbook was seriously out of balance because she had subtracted in base eight. However, for writing computer programs, base eight turned out to be a useful system.

The computer itself, though, did not actually operate in base eight. Instead, it operated in the binary system, which was based on the number *2* and used only two digits: *0* and *1*. In the binary system, the number *7* would be written *111*—a *4*, a *2*, and a *1*. Hopper's idea was to have the compiler translate the base eight code into binary. Although the binary system was no easier for programmers to work with than was octal, binary was more basic to the machine's own identity. The reason was that each switch had two possible positions: on or off. The "on" position corresponded nicely to the digit *1*, while the "off" setting assigned the switch a value of *0*. Using base eight or base ten would have required giving each switch a range of eight or ten possible settings: off, almost entirely off, mostly off, and so on. The gradations would have been difficult to distinguish and difficult to provide for technically. Thus, base two made the most sense.

What Hopper realized, though, was that *any* programming language could be translated into base two. Programmers did not have to use base eight just because doing so made sense to computer experts and mathematicians. In theory at least, programmers could write in base ten, even in English words and phrases, and the compiler could be instructed to translate that information into base two. The compiler, Hopper argued, could permit programmers to invent any language they chose—including ones that were much more user-friendly than the ones in operation for UNIVAC—and provide a means to convert that language into data the computer could understand.

Self-Programming

Second, and more powerfully, the compiler would instruct the computer to program itself—to find the subroutines it needed and to execute them. "Why start from scratch with every single program you write?" Hopper once demanded. "Develop one that would do a lot of the basic work over and over."[69] Hopper did this by assigning special call numbers to each of the subroutines she and her staff had compiled. The subroutines were then stored on the magnetic tape and fed into the computer, each with its call number attached.

Given a new program that contained the instruction "Find Subroutine #34," for example, the computer was supposed to translate the command into its own machine language, then search its memory for the specified subroutine. After executing that series of steps, the computer would then return to carrying out the steps in the remainder of the program. With enough subroutines stored in the computer's memory, programming would become a much easier task—and a much more accurate one as well.

Hopper's idea met with a great deal of skepticism. It was a wonderful plan, many of her colleagues agreed; however, most also thought it would never work. The particular problem, they believed, was the idea that a computer could program itself. In their view, computers could do arithmetic but nothing more. Hopper disagreed and set out to build a compiler anyway. Plunging ahead like this was one of Hopper's character traits. In her experience, asking for permission was risky; superior officers and bosses were apt to say no. "Go ahead and do it," she liked to say; "you can always apologize later."[70]

Building the compiler turned out to be fairly easy. Before long Hopper had constructed a device that she called the A-O. Today historians consider it the world's first automatic compiler, making Hopper its rightful inventor. Unfortunately for Hopper, convincing people that it actually worked was harder than devising the invention itself. She gave demonstrations of the compiler's speed and wrote new codes on demand, yet still she encountered resistance. In her estimation, acceptance took ten years—typical, she thought, where new ideas were concerned. The length of time, however, had little to do with developing the idea; in Hopper's view, that part of the process took only one of the ten years. As for the rest, she says pointedly, "The other nine years are needed to get people to believe it."[71]

COBOL

After the compiler, the next step was to write the business-friendly language that UNIVAC's owners hoped would make their machine a commercial success. Again, Hopper was in the forefront of this work. Knowing that words, not numbers, would be central to the success or failure of the machine in the business world, Hopper

Hopper developed a new computer language called Flow-matic which consisted of words instead of numbers.

began by writing several hundred typical programs and looking for verbs common to all of them. Words such as *add, stop,* and *execute* came up frequently, which gave Hopper an insight into how to write this new programming language.

By 1957 Hopper had developed a new language, called Flow-matic, which consisted of nothing but words. "This time," one writer notes dryly, "it took her three years to convince people"[72] of its effectiveness. Flow-matic was the first language of its type, but not the last. In short order, two other companies came out with competing languages of their own. Three languages were enough to prove that word-based programs could work. Three languages also gave consumers a choice. However, this sort of fragmentation had a significant disadvantage, too—data stored on one computer using one language would be unreadable by another operating system.

Once again, Hopper had an answer. She helped convene a group of computer experts to talk about possibilities for standardization. Out of that meeting came a commitment to devising a language that could be used by all computer manufacturers. The result was a language called COBOL, which was more or less an acronym for Common Business-Oriented Language.

Although Hopper was not a working member of the committee charged with creating COBOL, committee members freely acknowledged their debt to her. Her leadership in pushing for a common language was important in getting COBOL produced. So was the example of Flow-matic, along with many of the individual ideas that Hopper had used in her writing of the original computer language. When COBOL became widely accepted in the business community—after a somewhat rocky start—Hopper became known as "the Mother of COBOL." Years later, when she was approaching the age of eighty, that phrase was refined somewhat. "My crew call me Grandma COBOL,"[73] she told her college alumni magazine.

Later Years

Hopper was never one to rest on her laurels. After completing work on COBOL, she moved on to several new computer-related projects. In an era during which much of the emphasis was on machinery and technological advances, she recognized the importance of developing good software packages and fought hard for the inclusion of useful programs when computers were sold. She helped standardize the languages of U.S. Navy computers, and she was a pioneer in the use of computers to forecast the weather. Hopper also was instrumental in increasing the size of computer memory through a process known as virtual storage.

Neither was Hopper one to slow down as she aged. "I don't think I will ever be able to really retire," she said in the late 1980s. "I've always liked to work with either my head or my hands. I'm not content being a spectator."[74] Hopper continued to serve the military in various capacities until 1986, when she retired with the rank of a rear admiral. That year, at the age of eighty, she was appointed a senior consultant for the Digital Equipment Corporation, one of several positions in private industry that Hopper held throughout her life. She died on January 1, 1992, still hard at work making computers as easy to use as possible.

Recognition

For many years the value of Hopper's work was not widely recognized. Several early histories of computer technology leave her out more or less entirely, and most nonspecialists would have found her name unfamiliar well into the 1970s. But during the 1980s that began to change. As computer technology became more and more widespread, attention became focused on the people who had helped make computers a reality. Those who looked back saw that Grace Hopper was near the center of the computer revolution. Accolades began to pour in. Hopper was elected to the Engineering

Following her retirement from the navy, Hopper served as a senior consultant for the Digital Equipment Corporation.

Hopper's contributions to computer science were not widely recognized until the 1980s.

and Science Hall of Fame, was awarded the U.S. Navy Distinguished Service Medal, and received dozens of honorary degrees from various universities.

The attention was well deserved. From her invention of the compiler to the work she did on the development of COBOL, from the Mark I to UNIVAC, Hopper helped to make computers into the powerful machines they are today. More than that, she worked to make computing technology and languages accessible to the average person—a fact appreciated by anyone today who makes a purchase in a store, uses a word processor to write an essay, or goes on-line to do research on the Internet.

CHAPTER 5

Margaret Knight

Some inventors come to invent almost by accident. Like Rose O'Neill with her Kewpies, their creations are one of a kind, the product of a happy coincidence or an uncharacteristic brainstorm. Others, following the lead of computer expert Grace Hopper, set out to follow one career that has nothing to do with invention and then are abruptly assigned a task that sends them on an entirely different path. And some, such as animal specialist Temple Grandin, must overcome extremely long odds to create a place for themselves in the world—let alone to carve themselves a niche and a reputation as an inventor.

Some inventors, on the other hand, are almost driven to invent. These are the tinkerers, the experimenters, the dreamers—those who are drawn to pose questions and to seek out more efficient ways of accomplishing ordinary tasks. Most of the best-known women inventors fit into the accidental model, but a few do not. Among those who do not is Margaret Knight.

There are a good many question marks about Knight's life. Little is known of her childhood, and still less of what she did in her twenties. But enough evidence exists to make it clear that she was a tinkerer and an inventor at heart. The creator of many mechanical inventions, Knight did not live in a time and place when girls were encouraged to invent. Despite the pressure on her to conform to more "womanly" standards, Knight nevertheless spent most of her life doing what she liked to do best.

In the Mill

Margaret Knight was born in York, Maine, on February 14, 1838, but she grew up mainly in Manchester, New Hampshire. Manchester was home to many textile factories, all of which employed children and teenagers during Knight's childhood. In fact, some of these factories preferred to hire young people. For one thing, children were often willing to work for lower wages than their adult counterparts. For another, they were able to do some mill jobs better than older, larger people. Children especially came in handy for carrying out delicate jobs in tight places. Tying together bits of thread was one example; so was sliding under enormous looms to oil the moving parts.

Knight was no exception. By the age of twelve, perhaps earlier, she was hard at work in the mills. So were her brothers. The Knight family needed every cent it could earn, and the children's labor was necessary for survival. Despite the many hours of repetitive work in the cotton factories, however, Knight did have some time for play. Her interests, however, were not considered appropriate for girls of the time. She explained years later,

> As a child, I never cared for things that girls usually do; dolls never possessed any charms for me. I couldn't see the sense of coddling bits of porcelain with senseless faces; the only things I wanted were a jack-knife, a gimlet and pieces of wood. My friends were horrified. I was called a tomboy; but that made little impression on me. I sighed sometimes, because I was not like other girls; but wisely concluded that I couldn't help it, and sought further consolation from my tools.[75]

Like these two young boys, Margaret Knight and her brothers worked in a cotton factory as children.

Though Knight was not accepted by some of the other girls in the community, she found herself sought after by many of the local boys. The reason was simple enough: Margaret Knight, nicknamed "Mattie," was a skilled whittler and carver who produced beautiful toys, sleds, and other play equipment. This ability was especially prized in the 1840s, a time when store-bought goods were a luxury and few families could afford elaborate playthings. "I was always making things for my brothers," Knight later recalled. "[If] they [wanted] any thing in the line of playthings, they always said, 'Mattie will make them for us.' I was famous for my kites, and my sleds were the envy and admiration of all the boys in town."[76]

Most children who worked in the mills enjoyed—if only briefly—the sense of satisfaction that came with having a steady paycheck, however small. Once the novelty of having an income wore off, though, these children settled down to the drudgery of doing the same work over and over every day. For Knight, however, the factory was an interesting place. The work may have been hard, but the machinery was fascinating. Indeed, by the time she was twelve Margaret Knight had already demonstrated how intriguing she found machines—and how creatively she was able to think about them.

Knight's First Invention

Knight's first invention was sparked by an accident that occurred in the mill where she and her brothers worked. Injuries were common in the factory. The frenetic pace, the heavy machinery, and the oil that so often leaked onto the floor all created accidents. Weariness, inattention, and carelessness on the part of the workers also played a role in the number of employees who were hurt. One particular incident, however, was especially unsettling. The factory used long steel-tipped shuttles as part of the process of weaving cloth. Threads were attached to the shuttle, which then slid in and out of the cross threads. Somehow, while a shuttle was being used one day, it spun off the loom and flew across the room. The tip pierced and seriously injured a worker.

Though Knight was no more than twelve years old at the time, she immediately tackled the problem of how to prevent such accidents. Within a few weeks she had succeeded. The exact form of this first invention is not known today. Some evidence suggests that it was a device that automatically shut down the machine when a thread broke, preventing the mechanism from skidding the shuttle off in random directions. Other accounts argue that it may instead have been a cover or attachment of some kind, preventing the shuttle from moving beyond the edge of the loom. What we do know is that Knight was celebrated for her work. At least one writer of the time credited Knight with having affected the way cotton mills carried out safety procedures, and several others noted that her invention became a standard feature on many looms.

Whatever the invention looked like, it is evident that Knight solved the problem of restraining the shuttle through observation and careful thought, not through any kind of specialized training. Like many other children in New England during that time, Knight did not have much formal education, although how much she received is unclear. To judge from the standards of the era, it seems very likely that she completed sixth grade, possible that she completed eighth, and conceivable that she may have had some high school experience. Certainly she did not go beyond high school. Her education was sufficient to teach her the basics of reading, writing, and mathematics; however, that was all. With her safety device and all future inventions, Knight seems to have been entirely self-motivated and self-taught.

Many of Knight's contemporaries at the mill would have remained there throughout their lives. Knight—again for reasons unclear—did not. Beginning in her late teens, she held a succession of small jobs, including engraving, home repair, photography, and more. Knight had unspecified health problems during some of this

Until the middle of the nineteenth century, paper bags were not widely used.

time, too, which motivated her to move in with one of her brothers and do housekeeping chores for him. In 1867, her health not much improved, she moved to Springfield, Massachusetts, where she took a job with a business called the Columbia Paper Bag Company.

Paper Bags

Paper bags are such a part of today's world that it is easy to take them for granted. But back in 1867 they were hardly as important as they are now. Stores were smaller then, and less widespread. The population was more rural. Americans were accustomed to making things for themselves, or doing without,

76

rather than heading down to the nearest market. Bags of all kinds were less common and less vital to commerce than they are today.

Moreover, the market for paper bags in 1867 was relatively small. Most people owned cloth bags, usually made from burlap or other coarse fabrics. A shopper in the 1860s was much more likely to bring one of these bags to a store and ask a merchant to fill it than to expect to be given a disposable one. Cloth bags had several advantages, too. For one, they were sturdy. For another, they could be used again and again. Finally, they were fairly cheap. However, it is fair to say that the greatest advantage of the cloth bag of the 1860s was that it was not made out of paper. Paper bags, such as those made by Margaret Knight's new employer, were thin and flimsy, and no one who wanted to carry anything of any significant size dared to use one.

The basic problem with the production of paper bags was a financial one. To produce a paper bag cheaply enough to make a profit, bag companies had only one real design option: They had to cut, fold, and glue paper into a shape rather like a large mailing envelope of today. At its bottom, the bag was held together only with a fold or a dollop of paste. At its top, there was one narrow opening. A similar bag design is still used today for small items in drugstores and stationery supply shops, especially for greeting cards, postcards, and keychains.

This type of bag was easy enough to manufacture. Indeed, the process could be done mostly by machine. Unfortunately, the small capacity and the weakness of the bag's bottom made the bag impractical for anything much larger than a few sheets of paper. That eliminated the possibility of using it for groceries, certain dry goods, or for clothing.

Bag makers did have a competing design that they sometimes used. Called the square-bottomed style, it was much more similar to the paper grocery bags in common use today. Constructed with a wide opening, the bag folded for easy storage. Most importantly, the bottom was rectangular and was reinforced throughout with glue. The square-bottomed design was much more useful and would have been better received than the standard envelope style. However, the square-bottomed bags had to be folded and glued by hand—an arduous process, and one that added so much to the cost of the product as to make it too expensive to purchase.

Guide Fingers and Plate-Knife Folders

To Margaret Knight, the solution was obvious: build a machine that could do some of the work to create a square-bottomed bag. Accordingly, she put her mechanical skills to use. Her job at the

Columbia Paper Bag Company was not as demanding on her time or energy as most cotton mill jobs, and so in 1867 she began to study the problem. "I had plenty of leisure time for making observations," she wrote years later, "and such time was employed in watching the movement of the machines, and the manufacture of the square bottom bags by hand."[77] Each day she returned home and considered possible ways of constructing a machine that would fold and glue square bottoms onto bags.

Knight's colleagues and employers were not certain what to make of her dedication to

Margaret Knight worked on several models of a machine designed to produce a square-bottomed, brown paper shopping bag.

solving this problem. Others had tried without success to devise a similar machine, and some feared it was an impossible task. As her experiments progressed, the owner of the company even rebuked her for spending so much company time on the project. However, Knight's determination and ingenuity soon won over many of her colleagues. Her boss also withdrew his concern when he found out how far she had actually come—especially when Knight suggested that she might be willing to sell him the rights to the completed invention.

Although historians know relatively little about Knight's life, they do know a surprising amount about the process through which Knight built a machine that actually worked. The reason is that she kept detailed notebooks and diaries outlining her thoughts. These notebooks included sketches, comments, and other bits of information revealing her ideas. One of her diaries, for example, references a "guide finger and a plate-knife folder,"[78] among several other pieces of machinery that would ultimately appear in the finished product. Perhaps more important, the notebooks also demonstrate Knight's constant tinkering and positive attitude toward her work. "Heigh ho," she wrote at one point about a particularly sticky problem, "can't see how to turn that fold back—unless. . . ."[79] She was determined to succeed.

During the next two or three years Knight spent as much time as she could creating a machine that would actually produce square-bottomed bags. She produced one model after another, each made from wood or metal, and showed them to her colleagues and employers. The models were crude and often showed simply how one aspect of the process could be done: pasting without folding, folding without cutting, and so on. But in demonstrations, they seemed to do the job. One model, she said later, turned out "thousands of bags—not perfect bags, since they lacked the paste [but] good, handsome bags."[80] Buoyed by her success, Knight then took her model to a machinist's shop and asked him to build an iron version for her.

Patent Disputes

She would come to regret that decision. While the machinist worked, the model remained in his shop, on display to anyone who wandered inside. Knight had neglected to take out a patent on the machine, perhaps intending to wait until the machinist had finished his work. Most visitors would have given Knight's creation only a cursory glance and moved on, but one man did not. His name was Charles Annan. Annan evidently recognized the purpose of Knight's machine and appreciated its value. Annan made several visits to the machinist's shop on various pretexts, but his real intention was to gather information on the square-bottom bag maker. Working quickly, he constructed one much like Knight's and hastened to take out a patent on it.

Annan had no doubt expected that Knight would not make a fuss. If so, he was wrong. Furious, she hired a lawyer and filed suit for patent interference. The trial lasted sixteen days; each day's testimony cost Knight a hundred dollars in attorney fees and other expenses. She obviously felt strongly about the situation: Not only did she think she had a case, but she also believed that the money she spent would be more than made up for when the machine was perfected, marketed, and sold.

The Trial

The trial began in the fall of 1870. Knight's first order of business was to demonstrate her prior claim to the bag machine. She began by having her lawyer call the machinist as a witness. As Knight had hoped, he testified that Annan had seen Knight's model on numerous occasions. Knight's lawyer then attacked Annan's claim that her models were rickety, ineffective, and unrelated to Annan's work. Next, Knight produced her journals, along with several witnesses who testified that she had been working to develop a bag-making machine for at least two years. "I know what I saw,"

Knight's landlady told the judge, when asked whether Knight had been developing her ideas as early as February 1867. "I saw her making drawings continually . . . always of the machine. She has known nothing else, I think."[81]

On these points, Knight's evidence was clear and her argument strong. There was no reasonable case to be made that the idea was originally Annan's. Annan, however, then switched gears and argued that Knight had waited too long to file for a patent. Although by then it was apparent that Annan had taken Knight's idea, it was not clear that he was acting outside the law by doing so. Technically, Knight had to patent her ideas in order to claim them and to prevent others from using them. Although the law allowed a grace period between the working out of the idea and the patenting of it, Annan argued that Knight had waited well beyond the grace period.

The patent official who heard the case ultimately ruled against Annan. Conceding that Knight probably should have filed earlier, the official nevertheless determined that she had taken reasonable precautions to safeguard her interests. He also gave her the benefit of the doubt because she was a woman. Had Knight been a "man of business," the patent official explained, Annan's claim would have been accepted; because she was not, she could not have been expected to know and follow all the rules. "Considering her little practical acquaintance with machinery," he added, "her success in overcoming the many difficulties encountered is a matter of great surprise."[82]

Either the examiner had not actually paid much attention to the trial or he had already made up his mind that women were incapable of understanding machinery. During the trial, Knight had explained both her extensive experience with machines and the thought processes that went into building this one. "I have from my earliest recollection been connected in some way with machinery," she had told the court. "I have worked at almost everything where machinery is employed."[83] Insults aside, though, Knight had to be pleased. Against the odds, she had taken on Annan and had won the case. She was free to patent her invention, and she did.

The Effects of the Bag Machine

Knight's next step was to go into business for herself to perfect and market her machine. To do this, she joined forces with a Massachusetts businessman. Together, they started their own paper bag company in Connecticut. Though Knight was not involved in the day-to-day running of the factory, she nevertheless was part owner of the business and shared in the profits. She benefited in another way, too: the company paid twenty-five hundred dollars up front for the right to use her design, and it agreed to pay her a royalty ranging from five to twenty-five cents for every bag produced. Although it is unclear how much money she earned from this arrangement, there is no doubt that she was pleased with the deal.

It is also evident that sales of paper bags, in general, began to soar. According to estimates of the time, the machine could do the work of thirty people. With labor costs slashed, suddenly it became possible to create a bag with a square bottom at a price people were willing to pay. The impact of Knight's invention echoes today. "Every shopper who loads up at the supermarket," writes one modern-day observer, "is indebted to her."[84]

More recently, plastic bags have begun to overtake paper grocery bags in popularity. Still, the influence of Knight's invention persists. Shoppers today expect sturdy, cheap bags that can be disposed of easily, and few would accept anything less.

Knight's machine made it possible for sturdy paper bags to be mass-produced at a cost that supermarkets could afford.

More Inventions

The paper bag machine was Margaret Knight's first patent and most famous invention, but it was by no means her last. When she died in 1914, at the age of seventy-six, she left behind an array of inventions, nearly all of them connected in some way with machinery. Many had to do with shoes. Knight worked in the shoe industry for quite some time. She held four patents for various types of machines that would cut soles and another patent for a feeder that brought the raw materials into these machines.

Later in her life Knight became fascinated by engines, a relatively new technology, and earned another eight patents in that field. Her work in this area led her to produce a type of engine that she called the Knight Silent Motor. The motor may have been an innovation, but it does not seem to have been a financial success. Knight also developed a formula for nonskid tire tread—one of several inventions involving rubber, a great interest of hers throughout her inventing career. All of these inventions had some use, and many also represented breakthroughs of one kind or another. But it is fair to say that none of her later patents had the impact of the paper bag maker.

No one knows exactly how many devices Margaret Knight invented during her lifetime. Estimates have ranged from the low twenties to more than a hundred. Depending on whether improvements to already-existing inventions are included, Knight was the holder of between twenty and thirty patents. These were held either alone or in conjunction with male inventors, usually relatives or coworkers. There is also speculation, however, that Knight sold some of her invention ideas to other people, allowing them to patent the device under their own names in exchange for cash.

In addition, Knight apparently chose not to patent a number of her inventions, although her reasons for this decision are unclear. Perhaps she felt that some of her ideas were commercially unfeasible or had such a limited range of uses as to make them very nearly so. In either case, pursuing a patent may not have been worth the bother. Patenting also requires the inventor to reveal the full workings of a device, which Knight may have been reluctant to do. "Sometimes," a biographer points out, "an inventor's most important and potentially profitable inventions are kept as trade secrets rather than patented."[85]

Regardless, Knight's own count of her inventions, patented and unpatented, was somewhere between eighty and ninety. In 1913, the year before she died, an out-of-town journalist interviewed her and reported that she was "working twenty hours a day on her eighty-ninth invention."[86] Her obituary in the Framingham, Massachusetts, newspaper, where she had lived for the last twenty years of her life, gave a similar figure.

Besides being prolific, Knight was a bit of a curiosity. Often described as a professional inventor, Knight spent many years living in suburban Boston and working in what she called an inventing—or experimenting—office downtown. She had a small circle of friends, but she does not appear to have had an active social life. She never married, and she seems to have been mainly devoted to her work. All of this was unusual enough for a woman in the later years of the nineteenth century; it was even more unusual given that Knight's area of interest was machinery, a most decidedly unladylike passion.

"It Is a Genuine Gift"

But then, those who knew her accepted her enthusiasms, even if they did not always understand them. "She knows as much about machinery as though she had made it a study all her life," explained a contemporary. "It is a genuine gift; and she can no more help making machinery than [Civil War–era lecturer] Anna Dickinson can help making speeches."[87]

Knight herself seems to have been reasonably satisfied with her life, though she had a few regrets about the way the world at large perceived her. "I'm not surprised at what I've done," she told a reporter a few years after patenting her paper bag machine. "I'm only sorry I couldn't have had as good a chance as a boy, and been put to my trade regularly."[88] As her somewhat checkered employment history shows, finding jobs that matched her talents was often difficult for Knight, and it remained so until near the end of her life.

In many ways Margaret Knight was careful with her money and was a good entrepreneur. She tried to keep the rights to those inventions that appeared to be most profitable while selling the rights for those that looked less so. She had a reputation, no doubt stemming from the court battle over the paper bag maker, as a hard-nosed bargainer who knew the value of her work. On at least one occasion, Knight kept a small stake in an invention, sold the remaining rights to a well-financed company, and watched proudly as her part of the investment turned into a major moneymaker.

Knight's decisions however, did not always bring financial success. The Knight Silent Motor, for which she and a nephew jointly held patent rights, turned out to be worthless. And sometimes her work, once sold, turned out to be more valuable than she had anticipated. Late in life, Knight seems to have given up regular employment in other fields in favor of full-time inventing, a decision that may have led to more satisfaction but did not necessarily increase her wealth. In the end, Knight's money management skills were a wash. When she died in 1914, she left her heirs a few patents—most of them long since having ceased to earn any money—along with two bank accounts worth a total of $187.05, and $58 worth of furniture.

Toward the end of Knight's life, she did begin to reap some of the attention she had long deserved. She appeared as the subject of several newspaper and magazine interviews. The newspaper in her adopted hometown of Framingham, in particular, showed its pride at having an inventor in its area of coverage. Knight also began to attract notice from women's groups, especially those with a moderately feminist agenda. They held her up as an example of what a woman could accomplish despite the odds and despite the doubters.

Indeed, Knight's ultimate importance was measured neither in money nor even in the impact of the paper bag machine she invented and successfully marketed. Instead, she was proof that a woman could do well in a field traditionally reserved for men. Her work with machinery demonstrated the depth of her intuition, creativity, and understanding of mechanical principles. Her success was achieved despite the lack of other women following the same path, the handicap of little formal education, and the widespread doubt that a woman could—or would want to—learn about heavy machinery. In the end, the girl who was scorned for preferring jackknives and kite making to dolls became a pioneer and a role model whose story has been an example for hundreds of other girls with similar passions.

NOTES

Introduction: Women Who Invent

1. Quoted in Ethlie Ann Vare and Greg Ptacek, *Mothers of Invention*. New York: Quill, 1987, p. 31.

2. Quoted in Anne L. Macdonald, *Feminine Ingenuity*. New York: Ballantine Books, 1992, p. xx.

Chapter 1: Temple Grandin

3. Temple Grandin, *Thinking in Pictures and Other Reports from My Life with Autism*. New York: Doubleday, 1995, p. 43.

4. Quoted in Oliver Sacks, "An Anthropologist on Mars," *New Yorker*, December 27, 1993, p. 110.

5. Quoted in Sacks, "An Anthropologist on Mars," p. 106.

6. Grandin, *Thinking in Pictures and Other Reports from My Life with Autism*, p. 57.

7. Grandin, *Thinking in Pictures and Other Reports from My Life with Autism*, p. 31.

8. Grandin, *Thinking in Pictures and Other Reports from My Life with Autism*, p. 33.

9. Quoted in Kit Miniclier, "Autism Proves Gift for Visionary," *Denver Post*, February 21, 2000, p. B1.

10. Quoted in Sacks, "An Anthropologist on Mars," p. 112.

11. Grandin, *Thinking in Pictures and Other Reports from My Life with Autism*, p. 66.

12. Grandin, *Thinking in Pictures and Other Reports from My Life with Autism*, p. 19.

13. Quoted in Sacks, "An Anthropologist on Mars," p. 124.

14. Grandin, *Thinking in Pictures and Other Reports from My Life with Autism*, p. 62.

15. Grandin, *Thinking in Pictures and Other Reports from My Life with Autism*, p. 63.

16. Grandin, *Thinking in Pictures and Other Reports from My Life with Autism*, p. 99.

17. Sacks, "An Anthropologist on Mars," p. 114.

18. Quoted in Sacks, "An Anthropologist on Mars," p. 115.

19. Grandin, *Thinking in Pictures and Other Reports from My Life with Autism,* p. 146.

20. Grandin, *Thinking in Pictures and Other Reports from My Life with Autism,* pp. 153–54.

21. Grandin, *Thinking in Pictures and Other Reports from My Life with Autism,* p. 155.

22. Quoted in Miniclier, "Autism Proves Gift for Visionary," p. B1.

23. Quoted in Ann Marsh, "A Kinder, Gentler Abbatoir," *Forbes,* July 6, 1998, p. 86+.

24. Grandin, *Thinking in Pictures and Other Reports from My Life with Autism,* p. 155.

25. Quoted in Marsh, "A Kinder, Gentler Abbatoir," p. 86+.

26. Quoted in Miniclier, "Autism Proves Gift for Visionary," p. B1.

Chapter 2: Madame Walker

27. Quoted in A'Lelia Bundles, "Madam C. J. Walker—Cosmetics Tycoon," *Ms.,* July 1983, p. 92.

28. Quoted in Bundles, "Madam C. J. Walker," p. 92.

29. Quoted in Kathy Lee Peiss, *Hope in a Jar: The Making of America's Beauty Culture.* New York: Metropolitan Books, 1998, p. 90.

30. Quoted in Peiss, *Hope in a Jar,* p. 216.

31. Quoted in Bundles, "Madam C. J. Walker," p. 92.

32. Quoted in Bundles, "Madam C. J. Walker," p. 92.

33. Quoted in Bundles, "Madam C. J. Walker," p. 92.

34. Quoted in Peiss, *Hope in a Jar,* p. 209.

35. Quoted in Peiss, *Hope in a Jar,* p. 221.

36. Quoted in Peiss, *Hope in a Jar,* p. 228.

37. Quoted in Bundles, "Madam C. J. Walker," p. 93.

38. Quoted in Bundles, "Madam C. J. Walker," p. 91.

39. Quoted in Darlene Clark Hine, ed., *Black Women in America.* Brooklyn, NY: Carlson, 1993, p. 1,213.

Chapter 3: Rose O'Neill

40. *Dictionary of American Biography,* rev. ed. New York: Scribner, 1957, p. 573.

41. Alexander King, "Kewpie Doll," *New Yorker,* November 24, 1934, p. 22.

42. Quoted in King, "Kewpie Doll," p. 24.

43. Quoted in *Cobblestone,* special issue on women inventors. June 1994, p. 22.

44. Quoted in Miriam Formanek-Brunell, ed., "The Story of Rose O'Neill." www.system.missouri.edu/upress/spring1997/formanek.htm.

45. Constance Eileen King, *The Collector's History of Dolls.* New York: St. Martin's, 1978, p. 566.

46. Rose O'Neill, "The Kewpies' Christmas Frolic," *Ladies' Home Journal,* December 1909, p. 28.

47. O'Neill, "The Kewpies' Christmas Frolic," p. 28.

48. O'Neill, "The Kewpies' Christmas Frolic," p. 28.

49. King, *The Collector's History of Dolls,* p. 2.

50. Quoted in Vare and Ptacek, *Mothers of Invention,* p. 98.

51. Quoted in King, *The Collector's History of Dolls,* p. 568.

52. Quoted in *Book Review Digest.* New York: H. W. Wilson, 1929.

53. King, "Kewpie Doll," p. 23.

54. Quoted in Vare and Ptacek, *Mothers of Invention,* p. 98.

55. King, "Kewpie Doll," p. 25.

56. Quoted in *Book Review Digest.* New York: H. W. Wilson, 1922.

57. Quoted in Formanek-Brunell, "The Story of Rose O'Neill."

Chapter 4: Grace Hopper

58. Quoted in Autumn Stanley, *Mothers and Daughters of Invention: Notes for a Revised History of Technology.* Metuchen, NJ: Scarecrow, 1993, p. 637.

59. Quoted in Robert Slater, *Portraits in Silicon.* Cambridge, MA: MIT Press, 1987, p. 220.

60. Quoted in Slater, *Portraits in Silicon,* p. 7.

61. Quoted in Slater, *Portraits in Silicon,* p. 11.

62. Quoted in Vare and Ptacek, *Mothers of Invention,* p. 226.

63. Quoted in Vare and Ptacek, *Mothers of Invention,* p. 185.

64. Quoted in Slater, *Portraits in Silicon,* p. 85.

65. Quoted in Jennifer Mossman, ed., *Reference Library of American Women.* Farmington Hills, MI: Gale Research, 1999, p. 328.

66. Quoted in Slater, *Portraits in Silicon,* p. 222.

67. Quoted in Vare and Ptacek, *Mothers of Invention,* p. 185.

68. Tom Lehrer, *Too Many Songs.* New York: Pantheon, 1981, p. 111.

69. Quoted in Vare and Ptacek, *Mothers of Invention,* p. 184.

70. Quoted in *Vassar Quarterly,* Spring 1989, p. 41.

71. Quoted in Stanley, *Mothers and Daughters of Invention,* p. 639.

72. Stanley, *Mothers and Daughters of Invention,* p. 639.

73. Margaret Treadwell Field, "Class of 1928 Notes," *Vassar Quarterly,* Fall 1982, p. 50.

74. Quoted in Vare and Ptacek, *Mothers of Invention,* p. 187.

Chapter 5: Margaret Knight

75. Quoted in Macdonald, *Feminine Ingenuity,* p. 51.

76. Quoted in Macdonald, *Feminine Ingenuity,* p. 51.

77. Quoted in Macdonald, *Feminine Ingenuity,* p. 54.

78. Quoted in Edward T. James, ed., *Notable American Women,* vol. 2. Cambridge, MA: Belknap, 1971, p. 340.

79. Quoted in Macdonald, *Feminine Ingenuity,* p. 54.

80. Quoted in Macdonald, *Feminine Ingenuity,* p. 54.

81. Quoted in Macdonald, *Feminine Ingenuity,* p. 55.

82. Quoted in Macdonald, *Feminine Ingenuity,* p. 55.

83. Quoted in Susan Bivin Aller, "A Lady in a Machine-Shop," *Cobblestone,* June 1994, p. 20.

84. Quoted in Macdonald, *Feminine Ingenuity,* p. 50.

85. Stanley, *Mothers and Daughters of Invention,* p. 523.

86. Quoted in Stanley, *Mothers and Daughters of Invention,* p. 523.

87. Quoted in Stanley, *Mothers and Daughters of Invention,* p. 525.

88. Quoted in John A. Garraty and Mark C. Carnes, eds., *American National Biography,* vol. 12. New York: Oxford University Press, 1999, p. 815.

FOR FURTHER READING

Books

Linda Jacobs Altman, *Women Inventors*. New York: Facts On File, 1997. Provides short biographical accounts of several women inventors. Most of Altman's subjects do not overlap with this book.

Charlene Billings, *Grace Hopper: Navy Admiral and Computer Pioneer*. Hillside, NJ: Enslow, 1989. A readable, detailed book about Hopper, including many good quotations.

Ellen Showell and Fred Amram, *Women Invent in America*. Peterborough, NH: Cobblestone, 1995. A history of women and their inventions in the United States.

Periodicals

A'Lelia Bundles, "Madam C. J. Walker—Cosmetics Tycoon," *Ms.*, July 1983.

Cobblestone, special issue on women inventors, June 1994.

Internet Sources

Miriam Formanek-Brunell, ed., "The Story of Rose O'Neill." www.system.missouri.edu/upress/spring1997/formanek.htm. Provides a brief biographical account of O'Neill's life and reproduces many of her illustrations.

Works Consulted

Books

Barbara Carlisle Bigelow, ed., *Contemporary Black Biography*. Detroit: Gale Research, 1994. Provides information about Madame Walker.

Book Review Digest. New York: H. W. Wilson, 1922 and 1929. Includes reviews of several of Rose O'Neill's literary works.

Dictionary of American Biography. Rev. ed. New York: Scribner, 1957. Contains thorough and thoughtful biographical sketches of several of the women appearing in this book.

Antonia Fraser, *A History of Toys*. New York: Delacorte, 1966. Provides information about toys and dolls throughout history.

John A. Garraty and Mark C. Carnes, eds., *American National Biography*. Vol. 12. New York: Oxford University Press, 1999. Includes sketches on Margaret Knight and others.

Temple Grandin, *Thinking in Pictures and Other Reports from My Life with Autism*. New York: Doubleday, 1995. An autobiographical account, focusing on Grandin's struggles to survive in a nonautistic world; also includes some useful information on her inventions and the process by which she created them.

Darlene Clark Hine, ed., *Black Women in America*. Brooklyn, NY: Carlson, 1993. Provides information about Madame Walker, including a thorough bibliography.

Edward T. James, ed., *Notable American Women*. Cambridge, MA: Belknap, 1971. This book contains biographies of many women important in American history, with a strong emphasis on those from the Northeast. It includes information on a few full- or part-time inventors.

Constance Eileen King, *The Collector's History of Dolls*. New York: St. Martin's, 1978. Contains information on dolls through the ages.

Tom Lehrer, *Too Many Songs*. New York: Pantheon, 1981. Songs by a mathematician turned comedian.

Anne L. Macdonald, *Feminine Ingenuity*. New York: Ballantine Books, 1992. The definitive work on American women who hold patents. It includes biographical information on several of the women in this book, along with many others; it also discusses more general issues regarding women who have tried their hand at inventing. It is well written, detailed, and readable.

Jennifer Mossman, ed., *Reference Library of American Women.* Farmington Hills, MI: Gale Research, 1999. Includes an informative article on Grace Hopper.

Charles Panati, *Panati's Parade of Follies, Fads, and Manias.* New York: HarperPerennial, 1991. An enjoyable and informative book; it includes brief information on Rose O'Neill and the Kewpie craze.

Kathy Lee Peiss, *Hope in a Jar: The Making of America's Beauty Culture.* New York: Metropolitan Books, 1998. A thoughtful book about the development of the cosmetics and hair-care businesses. Special attention is paid to Madame Walker and the circumstances surrounding her life and work.

Robert Slater, *Portraits in Silicon.* Cambridge, MA: MIT Press, 1987. Provides biographies of people important in the development of the computer. It includes a useful chapter on Grace Hopper along with valuable background information.

Autumn Stanley, *Mothers and Daughters of Invention: Notes for a Revised History of Technology.* Metuchen, NJ: Scarecrow, 1993. A long and often opinionated book with lots of information about women inventors.

Ethlie Ann Vare and Greg Ptacek, *Mothers of Invention.* New York: Quill, 1987. A breezy, journalistic account of many women inventors and their brainstorms. The information ranges from very scant to quite detailed.

Periodicals

Margaret Treadwell Field, "Class of 1928 Notes," *Vassar Quarterly,* Fall 1982.

Alexander King, "Kewpie Doll," *New Yorker,* November 24, 1934.

Ladies' Home Journal, various issues of 1909 and 1910.

Ann Marsh, "A Kinder, Gentler Abbatoir," *Forbes,* July 6, 1998.

Kit Miniclier, "Autism Proves Gift for Visionary," *Denver Post,* February 21, 2000.

Rose O'Neill, "The Kewpies and the Aeroplanes," *Ladies' Home Journal,* January 1910.

———, "The Kewpies and the Baby," *Ladies' Home Journal,* February 1910.

———, "The Kewpies' Christmas Frolic," *Ladies' Home Journal,* December 1909.

Oliver Sacks, "An Anthropologist on Mars," *New Yorker,* December 27, 1993.

INDEX

PICTURE CREDITS

ABOUT THE AUTHOR

Stephen Currie is the author of more than thirty books and many magazine articles. Among his nonfiction titles are Music in the Civil War, Birthday a Day, Problem Play, We Have Marched Together: The Working Children's Crusade, and Life in a Wild West Show. He is also a first and second grade teacher. He lives in upstate New York with his wife, Amity, and two children, Irene and Nicholas.